DEAR BRUTUS

Produced on October 17th, 1917, at Wyndham's Theatre, London, with the following cast of characters:

MR. DEARTH	Mr. Gerald du Maurier
MR. PURDIE	Mr. Sam Sothern.
MR. COADE	Mr. Norman Forbes.
MATEY	Mr. Will West.
LOB	Mr. Arthur Hatherton.
MRS. DEARTH	Miss Hilda Moore.
MRS. PURDIE	Miss Jessie Bateman.
MRS. COADE	Miss Maude Millett.
JOANNA TROUT	Miss Doris Lytton.
LADY CAROLINE LANEY	Miss Lydia Bilbrooke.
MARGARET	Miss Faith Celli.

SYNOPSIS OF SCENES

ACT I.—Lob's House.

ACT II.—The Wood.

ACT III.—The Same as Act I.

DEAR BRUTUS

ACT I

SCENE.—LOB'S *house—the drawing-room of Sinister Warren,* LOB'S *house in a remote part of England. It should be a shallow scene, because through open french windows at the back there must be a big view of the garden, not merely painted on cloth but occupying part of the stage. It is a beautiful flower-garden at midsummer. Nothing seen but flowers, and a fountain. There is a door* L. *down stage, and another door into the dining-room* R. *This latter has two steps leading up to it, and the upper part is glass with a curtain across it. The drawing-room is pretty and quaint, but not so odd as it perhaps ought to be.*

There is a round table C., *with chairs above it and on either side. A large settee down* R. *Above it, a small table with a bowl of flowers and a jug of water. Below the* R. *end of the windows, a stand with ashtray and matches. Up* L., *between the windows and the fireplace, a large armchair, facing diagonally up* R. *The fireplace in an angled recess up* L. *Below it, a desk and chair. There are bowls and vases of flowers on the table and the desk.*

(See the Ground Plan at the end of the book.)

The CURTAIN *rises on an empty stage, dark and unlit, though the time is late evening. This gives a striking view of the garden, which is bathed in moonlight. We see from the glass of the door* R. *that the dining-room is lit up. We have a glimpse of men standing at the table as this door is opened by* MR. PURDIE *to let the ladies come into the drawing-room, and there is chatter and laughter as they do so.*

First comes MRS. COADE, *who is a delightful sunny lady of about sixty. Next* MRS. DEARTH, *a woman of thirty-five, who can be fascinating and dangerous; who also is discontented, and despises her husband. Next a languid lady,* LADY CAROLINE LANEY. *She has a drawling, rather insolent manner, and considers herself superior to the others. Then* MRS. PURDIE, *a simple young wife, wistful, who knows her husband is fond of* JOANNA. *Lastly,* JOANNA TROUT, *who is sentimental but a good sort. They are groping in the dark except for the light from the dining-room. There is the usual modesty about going-first.*

MRS. PURDIE (*in the background*). Go on, Coady, lead the way.

MRS. COADE. Oh dear, I don't see why I should go first.

MRS. PURDIE. The nicest always goes first.

5

MRS. COADE (*descending the two steps*). It's a strange house if I'm the nicest !

MRS. PURDIE. It *is* a strange house !

MRS. DEARTH. Down with you, Mrs. Coade. Make way for the second nicest. (*Meaning herself.*)

(MRS. COADE *crosses to* L.C. MRS. DEARTH *behind her.* MRS. PURDIE *and* LADY CAROLINE *follow, the former to down* R.C., *and the latter to* C. *above the table.*)

JOANNA (*entering after the others*). I suppose that means I'm the nastiest. (*She comes to* R. *of the table.*)

(*So far we have seen them in the light of the dining-room ; now the dining-room door shuts and they are in darkness.*)

LADY CAROLINE. Don't shut the door. I can't see where the switch is.

MRS. DEARTH (*going up* L.). Over here.

(MRS. DEARTH *switches on the lights. The ladies, now sure they cannot be overheard, flock together like conspirators.*)

(*Moving down* L.) We mustn't waste another moment. We are all agreed, aren't we ?

JOANNA (*above the chair* R. *of the table*). Now is the time.

MRS. COADE (*to above the table, gleefully*). Yes, now if at all. But should we ?

MRS. DEARTH. Certainly. And at once, before the men come in.

MRS. PURDIE (*moving* R., *to the settee*). You don't think we should wait for the men ? They are quite as much in it as we are. (*She sits on the settee.*)

LADY CAROLINE (*languidly, moving down* L.C.). Lob would be with them. If the thing is to be done, it should be now. (*She sits on the chair* L. *of the table.*)

MRS. COADE (*though still beaming*). Is it quite fair to Lob ? After all, he is our host.

(MRS. DEARTH *turns to the desk and commences to write.*)

JOANNA (*coaxingly*). Of course it isn't fair to him. But let's do it, Coady.

MRS. COADE. Yes, let's do it.

MRS. PURDIE (*rising slightly, and looking* L., *seeing that* MRS. DEARTH *is writing*). Mrs. Dearth *is* doing it !

(*They all look at* MRS. DEARTH—LADY CAROLINE *rising.*)

MRS. DEARTH (*writing*). Of course I am. The men are not coming, are they ?

(JOANNA *runs up* R. *and peeps through the glass of the dining-room door.*)

JOANNA. No. (*Returning to* R. *of the table.*) Your husband is having another glass of port.

MRS. DEARTH (*reading over what she has written*). I'm sure he is. One of you ring, please.

(JOANNA *presses the bell* R. *of the windows.*)

MRS. COADE. Poor Matey!

LADY CAROLINE. He wichly desewves what he is about to get. [*Her "r's" are thus pronounced throughout.*]

JOANNA (*glancing* L.). He's coming! Don't all stand huddled together like conspirators!

MRS. COADE. It's what we are! (*She sits above the table* C.)

(MRS. PURDIE *tries to sit* R. *of the table, but as* JOANNA *forestalls her, she snatches a book from the table, crosses* R., *and sits on the settee.* LADY CAROLINE, *who had moved to behind* MRS. DEARTH'S *chair, returns to* L. *of the table and sits.* MRS. DEARTH *is still sitting* L., *at the desk.*

MATEY, *a correct but furtive butler, enters down* L., *and is moving up towards the door* R. *when he is arrested, at* L.C., *by* MRS. DEARTH'S *voice.*

The ladies, though pretending to be uninterested, are very on the alert.)

MRS. DEARTH (*glancing up from her book, casually*). Matey, I wish this telegram sent.

MATEY (*moving* R. *of* MRS. DEARTH). Very good, ma'am. The village post office closed at eight, but if it is important . . .

MRS. DEARTH. It is. And you are so clever, Matey—I'm sure you can persuade them to oblige you.

MATEY (*pleased, taking the telegram*). I will see to it myself, madam. You can depend on its going.

(*There is a little gasp from* MRS. COADE—*the equivalent to dropping a stitch in needlework.*)

MRS. DEARTH. Thank you. (*Indifferently as* MATEY *makes to go.*) Better read it, Matey, to be sure that you can make it out.

MATEY (L.C.). Very good, ma'am.

(MATEY *reads the telegram and gets a shock. All are covertly watching.*)

MRS. DEARTH (*in a purring voice*). Read it aloud, Matey.

MATEY (*turning to her*). Oh, ma'am! (*He shudders.*)

MRS. DEARTH (*inexorably, without the purr*). Aloud!

MATEY (*reading huskily*). To Police Station, Great Commony.

Send officer first thing to-morrow morning to arrest Matey, butler, for theft of rings.

MRS. DEARTH (*calmly*). Yes, that's quite right. (*She picks up her book again.*)

(*All resume their pretended occupations.*)

MATEY (*to* LADY CAROLINE *imploringly*). My lady!

LADY CAROLINE (*languidly with her eyes on her book*). Shouldn't we say how many rings?

MRS. DEARTH. Yes, put in the number of rings, Matey.

(MATEY *makes mute appeals to one after the other but sees they are all relentless. He produces three rings from a secret place in his clothes and hands them in deathly silence to the various owners; one to* MRS. PURDIE, *one to* JOANNA *and one on desk to* MRS. DEARTH.)

MATEY (R. *of* MRS. DEARTH). May I tear this up, ma'am?

MRS. DEARTH. Certainly not. (*She takes the form.*)

LADY CAROLINE. I told you from the first that he was the culprit. I am never mistaken in faces, and I see broad arrows all over yours, Matey.

MATEY. It's deeply regretted.

MRS. DEARTH. I'm sure it is.

JOANNA (*rising*). We may as well tell him that it isn't our rings we are worrying about. (*To above* MRS. COADE'S *chair.*) They are just a means to an end, Matey.

MRS. DEARTH. Precisely. In other words, that telegram goes unless——

MATEY (*eagerly*). Unless?

(*They all suddenly abandon pretence of being otherwise occupied.* JOANNA *runs again to the dining-room door and peeps through.* MRS. PURDIE *comes to the chair* R. *of the table.*)

JOANNA (*returning to above and* R. *of* MRS. COADE, *and speaking with great emphasis*). Unless—unless—you can tell us instantly what peculiarity it is that all we ladies have in common.

(*All the ladies now have their eyes on* MATEY, *in whose face an uneasiness begins to grow.*)

MRS. PURDIE. Not only the ladies, the gentlemen as well. All Lob's guests in this house.

MRS. DEARTH (*with emphasis*). We have been here a week, and we find that when he invited us he knew us all so little that we began to wonder why he asked us. And now from word he has let drop we know that we were invited because of something—he thinks—we have—in common.

MRS. PURDIE. But he won't say what it is.

Mrs. Coade (*gurgling*). And we can't sleep at night, Matey, till we find out.

Joanna. And we are sure you know, and if you don't tell us—quod !

(*All these sentences have been fired at him quickly like pistol shots.*)

Matey (*whose uneasiness has increased*). I don't know what you mean, ladies.

(*We can see, however, that he does know.*)

Mrs. Dearth. Oh, yes, you do.

Mrs. Coade. You must admit that your master is a very strange person.

Matey (*with a gasp*). He is a little—odd, ma'am. That's why everybody calls him just Lob—not Mr. Lob.

Joanna. He is so odd that it has got on my nerves that we have been invited here for some sort of horrid experiment.

(Matey *starts. All look at him.*)

(*To* Matey.) You look as if you thought so, too !

Matey. Oh, no, miss. I—he—you shouldn't have come, ladies—you didn't ought to have come.

Lady Caroline (*turning in her chair*). Shouldn't have come ? (*She motions him to step down* l.c.) Now, my man, what do you mean by that ?

Matey (*taking a pace down*). Nothing, my Lady—I—I just mean—why did you come if you are the kind he thinks ?

Mrs. Purdie. The kind he thinks ?

Mrs. Dearth. What kind does he think ? Now we're getting at it.

Matey (*wriggling*). I haven't a notion, ma'am.

Lady Caroline. Then it isn't necessarily our virtue that makes Lob interested in us ?

Matey. No, my lady—oh, no, my Lady.

(Mrs. Dearth *laughs.*)

Mrs. Coade. And yet, you know, he's rather lovable.

Matey (*eagerly*). He is, ma'am. He's the most lovable old devil I ever—I beg your pardon, my Lady.

Joanna. And yet it's true. I have seen him among his flowers, petting them, talking to them, coaxing them till they simply had to grow.

(*They look out at the garden.*)

Mrs. Dearth. It certainly is a divine garden.

Mrs. Coade (*looking out through the windows*). How lovely it is in the moonlight. Roses, roses, all the way. . . . (*Dreamily.*) It is like a hat I had once when I was young. . . .

Mrs. Dearth. Lob is such an amazing gardener, I believe he could even grow hats.

Lady Caroline. He's a wonderful gardener, but is one sure that that is nice at his age ? What is his age, man ?

Matey (*scared*). He won't tell, my Lady. I think he's frightened that the police would step in if they knew how old he is. (*Uneasily.*) They do say in the village that they remember him seventy years ago, looking just as he does to-day.

Mrs. Dearth. Rubbish !

Matey. Yes, ma'am ; but there are his razors.

Lady Caroline. Razors !

Matey (*turning to her, a trifle maliciously*). You won't know about razors, my Lady, not being married—as yet—excuse me. But a married lady can tell a man's age by the number of his razors. (*A little scared.*) If you saw his razors—there's a little world of them, from patents of the present day back to implements so horrible you can picture him with them in his hand— scraping his way through the ages.

Lady Caroline. Ages ? You amuse one to an extent. (*She motions him back.*) Was he ever married ?

Matey. He has quite forgotten, my Lady. How long ago is it since Merrie England ?

Mrs. Purdie. In Queen Elizabeth's time, wasn't it ?

Matey. He says he's all that's left of Merrie England, that little man !

Mrs. Dearth. Fiddle-de-dee !

Mrs. Purdie. Lob ! I think there is a famous cricketer called Lob.

Mrs. Coade. Wasn't there a Lob in Shakespeare ?

(*Nobody knows or cares.*)

No, of course I'm thinking of Robin Goodfellow.

Lady Caroline. The names are so alike.

Joanna. Robin Goodfellow was Puck.

Mrs. Coade (*triumphant*). That's what was in my head. Lob was another name for Puck.

Joanna (*moving down* R.C.). Well, he's certainly rather like what Puck might have grown into if he had forgotten to die. (*Turning.*) And, by the way, I remember now he does call his flowers by the old Elizabethan names.

Matey. He always calls the nightingale Philomel, miss— if that is any help.

Mrs. Dearth. None whatever. Tell me this. Did he specially ask you all for Midsummer week ?

Ladies. Yes, yes.

Matey. He would !

Mrs. Coade. What do you mean ?

MATEY. He always likes them to be here on Midsummer night, ma'am.

MRS. DEARTH (*rising*). Them ? Whom ?

(*A tiny pause. Then* MATEY *speaks slowly and sombrely.*)

MATEY. Them who have that in common.

MRS. PURDIE. What can it be ?

MATEY (*dissembling*). I don't know.

LADY CAROLINE. I hope we are all nice women. We don't know each other very well. Does anything startling happen at these times ?

MATEY (*doggedly*). I don't know.

JOANNA. Why, I believe this is Midsummer Eve !

MATEY. Yes, miss, so it is. (*Grimly.*) The villagers know it. They are all inside their houses to-night—with the doors barred.

LADY CAROLINE. Because of—oh, *him* ?

MATEY. He frightens them. There are—stories.

MRS. DEARTH. What alarms them ? Tell us—or—— (*She brandishes the telegram.*)

MATEY. I know nothing for certain, ma'am ; I've never done it myself. He's wanted me to, but I wouldn't.

MRS. PURDIE. Done what ?

MATEY (*with fine appeal*). Oh, ma'am, don't ask me. (*To* MRS. DEARTH *and thoroughly believing what he says.*) Be merciful to me, ma'am. I'm not bad naturally. It was just going into service that did for me ! The accident of being flung among bad companions. It's touch and go how the poor turn out in this world ; all depends on your taking the right or the wrong turning.

MRS. COADE (*commiserating*). I daresay that's true.

MATEY (*turning to* MRS. COADE). When I was young, ma'am, I was offered a clerkship in the City. If I had taken it there wouldn't be an honester man alive to-day. I would give the world to be able to begin over again !

MRS. COADE. It's very sad, Mrs. Dearth.

MRS. DEARTH. I'm sorry for him, but still——

MATEY (*appealing to* LADY CAROLINE). What do you say, my Lady ?

LADY CAROLINE. As you ask me, I should certainly say jail !

MATEY (*to* MRS. DEARTH). If you'll say no more about this, ma'am (*indicating the telegram*), I'll give you a tip that's worth it.

MRS. DEARTH. Ah, now you're talking !

LADY CAROLINE. Don't listen to him !

MATEY. You're the one that's hardest on me.

LADY CAROLINE. Yes, I flatter myself I am.

MATEY. You might take a wrong turning yourself, my Lady.

LADY CAROLINE. I ? How dare you ?

(JOANNA *turns again to the dining-room door up* R.)

JOANNA. They're rising ! (*She returns to* R.C.)

MRS. DEARTH. Very well, we agree—if the tip is good enough !

LADY CAROLINE. You'll regret this !

MATEY (*to* MRS. DEARTH). Thank you, ma'am ! It's this : (*with sombre emphasis*) I wouldn't go out to-night if he asks you. Go into the garden, if you like. The garden's all right. I wouldn't go farther—to-night.

MRS. COADE. But he never proposes to us to go farther. Why should he to-night ?

MATEY. I don't know, ma'am, but don't any of you go (*to* LADY CAROLINE, *vindictively*)—except you, my Lady. I should like you to go.

LADY CAROLINE. Fellow !

(*They all look at one another and nod.*)

MATEY. Is that all, ma'am ?

MRS. DEARTH. I suppose so. (*She tears up the telegram.*)

MATEY. Thank you. (He moves down L.)

LADY CAROLINE. You should have sent that telegram off.

JOANNA. You are sure you have told us all you know, Matey ?

MATEY (*checking at* L.). Yes, miss.

(MRS. DEARTH *rises and moves to above and* L. *of the table.* MATEY *is about to exit, but turns at the door, coming in a pace.*)

(*Impressively.*) Above all, ladies, I wouldn't go into the wood.

MRS. PURDIE (*rising*). The wood ? Why, there is no wood within a dozen miles of here.

MATEY. No, ma'am. But—all the same—(*very slowly*) I wouldn't go into it, ladies—not if I was you !

(MATEY *turns and exits* L., *leaving the ladies puzzled.*)

JOANNA (*up* R.C.). Here's Lob !

(JOANNA *moves down* R. MRS. PURDIE *and* MRS. DEARTH *move up, below the* R. *window up* C. LADY CAROLINE *goes up below the* L. *window.* MRS. COADE *is above the table* C.

LOB *enters from the dining-room. He is rather unearthly, very small and exceedingly old, but very light and vivacious. He enters with portentous gravity, his hands behind his back, his head bent, and he crosses thus down to* L.C. *All withdraw a little as he enters. At* L.C. *he suddenly jumps completely round to face them, which gives them a start. He peers at them to see if they are amused. It has amused him vastly.*)

LOB (*to* MRS. COADE). Standing, dear lady ? Pray be seated.

(LOB *draws out the chair* L. *of the table, and as* MRS. COADE *is about to sit in it he pulls it away, almost from under her. She saves herself from falling by gripping the table. He sinks in the desk chair in a paroxysm of delight, kicking one leg in the air, which is a characteristic way of expressing delight in himself.* JOANNA *is at* R.C. MRS. DEARTH *moves down* R. *to the settee.* MRS. COADE, *much amused, aims a playful blow at* LOB *with her finger.*)

MRS. COADE. You monkey!

LOB (*chuckling gleefully, and bringing her the flowers from the desk*). It's quite a flirtation, isn't it ?

(LOB *crosses below the table and sits* R. *of it, with his legs beneath him, as like a ball as possible. Outside, the moonlight deepens, slowly and imperceptibly.*

JOANNA *and* MRS. DEARTH *sit on the settee and eye* LOB'S *back, suspiciously.* MRS. PURDIE *and* LADY CAROLINE *watch him from the windows.*

MR. COADE, *a happy, lazy old man, enters from the dining-room up* R., *smoking a cigarette.*)

COADE. Hope you've been missing us ! (*To the ladies.*) You are sure you don't mind ? (*Indicating his cigarette.*)

MRS. DEARTH. You know we like it, Mr. Coade.

(MR. PURDIE *enters* R. *after* COADE. *He is a young barrister, and is modestly sure that he is of a deeply passionate nature.*)

Is my husband still sampling the port, Mr. Purdie ?

PURDIE (R.C.). Do you know, I believe he is—are the ladies willing, Coade ?

COADE (C.). I hadn't told them. (*Crossing to* MRS. COADE *solicitously.*) The fact is that I'm not sure whether it wouldn't tire my wife too much. Do you feel equal to a little exertion, Coady, to-night, or is your foot troubling you ?

MRS. COADE (*beaming as usual, for they are a happy pair*). No, Coady, I have been resting it.

COADE. That's right. (*He gets a footstool for her from the fireplace, and places it for her.*) There ! Don't disturb it for a while, as we are going out for a walk presently. (*He gets the chair from the desk, and sits* L. *of her.*)

MRS. COADE. Yes, let's go into the garden.

PURDIE. No, not the garden to-night. (*Towards the settee.*) We are going farther afield. (*Jocular, mysterious.*) We have an adventure on for to-night.

MRS. DEARTH. Oh ?

PURDIE. Get thick shoes and a wrap, Mrs. Dearth—indeed, all of you.

LADY CAROLINE. Where do you propose to take us ?

PURDIE. To find a mysterious wood.

LADIES. A wood ?

(MRS. PURDIE *and* LADY CAROLINE *come down above the table* R.C. *quickly. They take a sharp look at* LOB, *who is exaggeratedly innocent.*)

JOANNA. Is it your fun, Mr. Purdie ? You know quite well that there are not any trees for miles around. You have said yourself that it is the one blot on the landscape.

COADE (*jocularly solemn*). Ah, on ordinary occasions, but allow me to point out to you, Miss Joanna, that this is Midsummer Eve.

(*The ladies again look sharply at* LOB, *who is wickedly innocent.*)

PURDIE. Tell them what you told us, Lob. (*At the back of* LOB, *pulling his ears.*)

LOB. It's all nonsense, of course—just foolish talk of the villagers. (*Like one pitying their credulity.*) They say that on Midsummer Eve there is a strange wood in this part of the country.

MRS. DEARTH. Where ?

PURDIE. Ah, that is one of its most charming features. It is never twice in the same place, apparently. It has been seen on different parts of the Downs and on More Common—once it was close to Radley village and another time about a mile from the sea ! Oh, a sporting wood !

LADY CAROLINE (*moving a little* L.C.). Lob is anxious we should all go and look for it ? (*She comes down* L. *of* COADE, *and turns.*)

COADE. Oh, no, Lob's the only sceptic in the house. Says it's all rubbish, and we'll be sillies if we go. But we believe, eh, Purdie ?

PURDIE (*moving to above the table* R. *of* MRS. PURDIE). Rather !

(MRS. PURDIE *moves to* L. *of the chair* C.)

LOB. Just wasting the evening. Let's have a round game at cards here instead.

PURDIE. No, sir, I am going to find that wood.

JOANNA. What's the good of it when it's found ?

PURDIE (*a pace or two* R.C.). We shall wander in it deliciously, listening to a new sort of bird called the Philomel.

MRS. DEARTH. Ah ! (*Another sharp look at* LOB.)

JOANNA (*rising*). All together ? (*She crosses to* PURDIE R. *of the table.*)

PURDIE. No, in pairs. (*He gives her a significant look.*)

(MRS. PURDIE *moves up* L. *to the fireplace.*)

JOANNA (*demurely*). I think it would be rather fun. Come on, Coady, I'll lace your boots for you, I'm sure your poor foot will carry you nicely. (*Crossing to the door* L.)

MRS. DEARTH (*rises, still suspicious*). Miss Trout, wait a

moment! (*She moves to* R. *of* LOB'S *chair*.) Lob, has this
wonderful wood any special properties ?

LOB. Pooh ! There's no wood.

LADY CAROLINE (*moving up* C., *above the table*). You've never
seen it ?

LOB. Not I. Don't believe in it.

MRS. DEARTH. Have any of the villagers ever been in it ?

LOB. So it's said ; so it's said.

MRS. DEARTH. What did they say were their experiences ?

LOB. That isn't known. They never came back.

JOANNA. Never came back ! (*She moves from the door to* L.C.)

LOB. Absurd, of course. You see, in the morning the wood
was gone, and so they were gone, too. (*This is rather creepy.*)

JOANNA (*to above, and between* MR. *and* MRS. COADE). You
know, I don't think I like this wood.

MRS. COADE. It certainly is Midsummer Eve.

COADE. Of course if you ladies are against it we'll drop the
idea. It was only a bit of fun.

MRS. DEARTH (*with a malicious eye on* LOB). Better give it
up—to please Lob.

PURDIE. Oh, all right, Lob. What about that game of
cards ?

COADE. Yes, yes. (*He rises.*)

(*Here* LOB *bursts into tears and sobs with disappointment. They
don't know what to do. He falls on his knees* R. *of the table,
and then creeps under it, where he sits forlorn.*)

LOB (*under the table*). I wanted you to go. I had set my
heart on your going. It's the thing I wanted, and it isn't good
for me not to get the thing I want.

MRS. COADE. Good gracious ! He's wanted it all the time !
You wicked Lob ! (*Looking under the table.*)

MRS. DEARTH. Now, you see there is something in it !

COADE. Nonsense, Mrs. Dearth, it's all a joke !

MRS. PURDIE (*kneeling,* R. *of the table, and coaxing* LOB).
Don't cry, Lobby.

LOB. Nobody cares for me—nobody loves me. And I need
to be loved.

(MRS. COADE *and* MRS. PURDIE, *joined by* JOANNA, *bend down
and make much of him.*)

JOANNA. Yes, we do, we all love you. Nice, nice Lobby.

MRS. PURDIE. Dear Lob, I'm so fond of you.

JOANNA. Dry his eyes with my own handkerchief.

LADY CAROLINE. Don't pamper him !

LOB. I need to be pampered !

MRS. COADE. You funny little man ! Let us go at once and
look for his wood.

MRS. PURDIE. Yes, let's.

JOANNA. Rather ! Shoes, cloaks, and hats forward ! (*Crossing* L.) Come on, Lady Caroline, just to show you're not afraid of Matey.

(LADY CAROLINE, PURDIE, MRS. PURDIE, *the* COADES, *and lastly* MRS. DEARTH *follow* JOANNA *off gaily* L., *chatting, dragging the reluctant ones.* COADE, *before his exit, replaces his chair at the desk.*

LOB, *left alone, gloats over his success in an uncanny way.* MRS. DEARTH *goes last, the only one who really suspects* LOB. *He suddenly sees her down* L., *watching him, and drops the flowers from the vase which he has taken from the table,* C. *To him, this is a tragedy. He utters long-drawn moans, then goes down on the floor, picking up the flowers, individually examining their hurts, pressing them to him as if they were children.*

MRS. DEARTH *exits* L.)

LOB (*to the flowers*). Poor bruised one, it was I who hurt you. Lob is so sorry. Lie there ! (*To another.*) Pretty, pretty, let me see where you have a pain ?—you fell on your head—is this the place ? Now I make it better. (*To another.*) Oh, little rascal, you are not hurt at all, you just pretend. (*To another, whose stem is broken.*) Oh dear, oh dear, sweetheart, don't cry. You are now prettier than ever. You were too tall. Oh, how beautiful you smell now that you are small. (*He rises with them in his arms.*) Drink, drink ! (*He puts them in another vase* R., *which has already some flowers in it.*) Now you are happy again. The little rascal smiles ! All smile, please—and nod heads—aha ! aha ! You love Lob—Lob loves you !

(MR. PURDIE *and* JOANNA *come in rather secretly by the window.* LOB *behaves as if he had caught them love-making ; he beckons to the flowers as if he had something funny to tell them, whispers some merry jest to them.*)

JOANNA (*up* C., L. *of* PURDIE) What were you saying to them, Lob ?

LOB (*turning, and going down* L.). I was saying "Two's company, three's none ! "

(LOB *exits grinning,* L., *with a final nod to the flowers.*)

JOANNA. That man—he suspects ! (*She goes* L.)

PURDIE (*following her to* L.C.). Who minds him ? (*Lovingly ; above her.*) Joanna !

JOANNA (*moving to below the chair* L. *of the table*). And Mabel ? She saw you kiss my hand. I can't quite make her out. She was so deadly quiet about it. (*Facing* PURDIE, *who is now on her* L.) Oh, Jack, if Mabel suspected !

PURDIE. There's nothing for her to suspect !

JOANNA (*comforted*). No, there isn't, is there ? Jack, I'm not doing anything wrong, am I ?

PURDIE (*taking her hand fondly*). You ?

JOANNA (*giving him her other hand also*). Mabel is your wife, Jack. I should so hate myself if I did anything that was disloyal to her.

PURDIE. Those eyes could never be disloyal—my lady of the nut-brown eyes !

JOANNA. Ah, Jack ! All I want is to—to help her and you.

(*Both are believing all they say.*)

PURDIE. I know—how well I know—my dear brave love !

JOANNA. I'm very fond of Mabel, Jack. I should like to be the best friend she has in the world.

PURDIE (*pressing her to him*). You are, dearest ! No woman ever had a better friend.

JOANNA (*in his embrace*). And yet I don't think she really likes me—I wonder why ?

PURDIE. It's just that Mabel doesn't understand. Nothing would make me say a word against my wife——

JOANNA. I wouldn't listen to you if you did.

PURDIE. I love you all the more, dear, for saying that. But Mabel is a cold nature and she doesn't understand.

JOANNA. She doesn't appreciate your finer qualities.

PURDIE. That's it. (*He kisses her hand and crosses below her to R.C., speaking with gloomy satisfaction.*) I often think, Joanna, that I am rather like a flower that has never had the sun to shine on it nor the rain to water it. (*He sits on the lower arm of the chair R. of the table.*)

JOANNA (*sitting L. of the table*). You almost break my heart.

PURDIE (*almost cheerful at the thought*). I suppose there is no more lonely man than I walking the earth to-day.

JOANNA. It's so mournful !

PURDIE. It is the thought of you that sustains me, elevates me. You shine high above me like a star.

JOANNA. No, no ! I wish I was wonderful, but I'm not.

PURDIE. You have made me a better man, Joanna.

JOANNA. I am so proud to think that.

PURDIE. You have made me kinder to Mabel.

JOANNA. I am sure you are always kind to her. (*She sits c. of the table.*)

PURDIE. Yes, I hope so. (*He rises and turns up R.C.*) But I think now of special little ways of giving her pleasure. (*With sudden vehemence crossing to L.C., above the table.*) That never-to-be-forgotten day when we first met, you and I ! (*He comes down and kneels L. of her chair.*)

JOANNA. That tragic, lovely day by the weir ! Oh, Jack !

B

Purdie (*carried away by the beauty of his conduct*). Do you know how in gratitude I spent the rest of that day ?

Joanna. Tell me.

Purdie. I read to Mabel aloud for an hour. I did it out of kindness to her, because I had met you.

Joanna. It was dear of you.

Purdie. Do you remember that first time my arms—your waist—you are so fluid, Joanna. (*The fluidity of her is so great that it is almost a pain to think of it.*) I gave her a ruby bracelet for that.

Joanna. It is a gem. You have given that lucky woman many lovely things.

Purdie. It's my invariable custom to go straight off and buy her something whenever you have been sympathetic to me. Those new earrings of hers—they are in memory of the first day you called me Jack. Her gown—the one with the beads—was because you let me kiss you.

Joanna. I didn't exactly let you.

Purdie. No, but you have such a dear way of giving in.

Joanna (*suddenly faintly disturbed*). Jack, she hasn't worn that gown of late.

Purdie. Nor the jewels either. I think she has some sort of idea now that when I give her anything nice it means that you have been nice to me. She has rather a suspicious nature, Mabel ; she never used to have it, but it seems to be growing on her. I wonder why, I wonder why, Joanna ? (*He kisses her solemnly.*)

(Mrs. Purdie *passes outside the french windows, sees them, and passes off sadly,* L. *to* R.)

Joanna (*rising*). Who was that ? (*She rises.*)

Purdie (*rises, and going up to the window*). There's no one.

Joanna. Yes, there was. (*Crossing* R., *and turning to face up* C.) If it were Mabel ! (Purdie *comes down* R.C.) Oh, Jack, if she saw us she will think you were kissing me.

Purdie (*kissing her again*). No, no !

(Purdie's *arms are about her when enter* Mrs. Purdie *quietly at the french windows up* C.)

Mrs. Purdie (*quietly*). I am so sorry to interrupt you, Jack, but please wait a moment before you kiss her again. Excuse me, Joanna.

(Mrs. Purdie *pulls the curtains and the garden is hidden from view, but she leaves the windows open.*)

I don't want the others to see. (*Crossing down* L.) They mightn't understand how noble you are, Jack. (*Turning at the door.*) You can go on now.

(MRS. PURDIE *exits* L.)

(NOTE.—*At this point, change the exterior setting to the wood.*)

JOANNA. How extraordinary! Of all the—— (*She crosses* L. *below the table.*) Oh, how contemptible! (*She calls.*) Mabel!

(MRS. PURDIE *comes back* L. PURDIE *comes down* R.)

MRS. PURDIE. Did you call me, Joanna?

JOANNA. I insist on an explanation. (*Rather haughty.*) What were you doing out there, Mabel?

MRS. PURDIE. I was looking for something I have lost!

PURDIE. Anything important?

MRS. PURDIE. I used to fancy it, Jack. It is my husband's love. You don't happen to have picked it up, Joanna? If you don't value it very much I should like it back—the pieces, I mean.

JOANNA. Mabel—I—I will not be talked to in that way. To imply that I—that your husband—oh, shame! (*She turns up* L.C.)

PURDIE. I must say, Mabel, that I am a little disappointed in you. I certainly understood that you had gone upstairs to put on your boots.

MRS. PURDIE. Poor old Jack! (*Bitingly.*) A woman like that!

JOANNA (*above the table*). I forgive you, Mabel! You will be sorry for this afterwards.

PURDIE. Not a word against Joanna, Mabel. If you knew how nobly she has spoken of you.

JOANNA (*to above the chair* R. *of the table*). She does know. She has been listening.

(*There is a gasp and a movement from* MRS. PURDIE. *The two ladies glare at each other, and for a moment there is danger of the scene degenerating into something worse; but* PURDIE *intervenes.*)

PURDIE (*crossing to* L.C. *below the table*). This is a man's business. I must be open with you, Mabel. It is the manlier way. If you wish it, I shall always be true to you in word and deed. It is your right. But I cannot pretend that Joanna is not the one woman in the world for me. If I had met her before you—it's Fate, I suppose. (*He turns up above the chair* L. *of the table.*)

JOANNA (*moving to below the chair* R. *of the table*). Too late! Too late! (*She sits in the chair.*)

MRS. PURDIE. I suppose you never knew what true love was till you met her, Jack?

PURDIE. You force me to say it. Joanna and I are as one

person. We have not a thought at variance. We are one rather than two.

Mrs. Purdie (*looking at* Joanna). Yes, and that's the one! (*Scornfully.*) I am so sorry to have marred your lives.

Purdie (*thinking himself rather fine*). If any blame there is, it is all mine, she is as spotless as—as—the driven snow. The minute I mentioned love to her she told me to desist.

Mrs. Purdie. Not she! (*She goes to the door* L. *and pauses.*)

Joanna (*rising*). So you *were* listening! (*She moves up* R.C.) Mabel, don't you see how splendid he is!

Mrs. Purdie. Not quite, Joanna.

(Mrs. Purdie *exits* L.)

(Purdie *moves up to the fire* L.)

Joanna (*crossing up* L.C. *to* Purdie). How fine of you, Jack, to take it all upon yourself.

Purdie (*nobly*). It is the man's privilege.

Joanna. Mabel has such a horrid way of seeming to put people in the wrong.

Purdie. Have you noticed that? Poor Mabel, it's not an enviable quality!

Joanna (*turning away, above the table* C. *Despondently*). I don't think I care to go out now. She has spoilt it all. She has taken the innocence out of it, Jack.

Purdie (*moving towards her*). You'll come, dear, surely, and we'll give the others the slip.

(*They move together a little* L.C.)

Joanna. If we do, Mabel will say we did it intentionally.

Purdie. We must be brave and not mind her. Oh, Joanna, if we had met in time! If only I could begin again! To be doomed for ever just because I once took the wrong turning—it isn't fair.

Joanna. The wrong turning! Now, who was saying that a moment ago—about himself? Why, it was Matey.

(*They hear something.*)

Purdie. Is that her come back again? It's too bad.

(Purdie *puts his arm around* Joanna *to face* Mrs. Purdie *boldly, but they look foolish when* Mrs. Dearth *enters* L. *in her cloak, etc.*)

Ah! It's you, Mrs. Dearth.

Mrs. Dearth. Yes, it is, but thank you for telling me, Mr. Purdie.

(Joanna *escapes from* Purdie's *arm, but he keeps it extended, not knowing that it does not still enfold her. She pulls it down.*)

I don't intrude, do I? (*She crosses below the table to* R.)

JOANNA (*barking*). Why should you ?

PURDIE. Rather not. We were—hoping it would be you. I can't think what has become of the others. We have been looking for them everywhere. . . . (*He glances vaguely round the room, as if they might so far have escaped detection.*)

MRS. DEARTH (*moving up* R.C.). Well, do go on looking— (*pointing to the table*) under that flower-pot would be a good place. It's my husband I am in search of. (*She moves to down* R.)

PURDIE (*moving* R.). Shall I rout him out of the dining-room ? (*He checks at* R.C.)

MRS. DEARTH (*with mock seriousness*). How too unutterably kind of you, Mr. Purdie. I hate to trouble you, but it would be the sort of service one never forgets.

PURDIE. You know I believe you are chaffing me.

MRS. DEARTH. No, no, I am incapable of that !

PURDIE (*glancing up* L.C. *at* JOANNA). I won't be a moment.

MRS. DEARTH. Miss Trout and I will await your return with ill-concealed impatience. (*She sits* R. *of the table.*)

(PURDIE *exits up* R., *into the dining-room.*)

(MRS. DEARTH *looks at* JOANNA *up* L.C., *who tosses her head.*)

(*As if reading* JOANNA'S *thoughts.*) Yes, I suppose you're right. I daresay I am.

JOANNA. I didn't say anything. (*Ready for a quarrel.*)

MRS. DEARTH. I thought I heard you say, " That hateful Dearth woman coming butting in where she's not wanted."

JOANNA (*tartly*). You certainly have good ears.

MRS. DEARTH. Yes, they have always been admired.

JOANNA. By the painters for whom you sat when you were an artist's model ?

MRS. DEARTH. So that has leaked out, has it ?

JOANNA (*rather ashamed*). I shouldn't have said that.

MRS. DEARTH. Do you think I care whether you know or not ?

JOANNA. I'm sure you don't. Still, it was cattish of me.

MRS. DEARTH. It was.

JOANNA (*flaring up*). I don't see it !

(MRS. DEARTH *laughs.*)

(JOANNA *stamps and exits* L.)

(MR. DEARTH *comes in* R. *He is a man of forty. An artist, his appearance gone a little to seed. He is not in the least intoxicated, but he is flushed with wine. A good man who has gone wrong, and in his heart despises himself for it. He is, in a quiet way, rather a wreck.*)

DEARTH (*coming to* C. *above the table*).   I'm uncommon flattered that you should want me, Alice.   It quite takes me aback.

MRS. DEARTH (*who despises him*).   It isn't your company I want, Will.

DEARTH.   You know, I felt that Purdie must have delivered your message wrongly.

MRS. DEARTH.   It is something to do with Lob.   I want you to come with us on this mysterious walk and keep an eye on him.

DEARTH.   On poor little Lob !   Oh, surely not !

MRS. DEARTH.   I can't make the man out.   I want you to tell me something.   When he invited us here, do you think it was you or me he especially wanted ?

DEARTH.   Oh, you.   He made no bones about it—said there was something about you that made him want uncommonly to have you down here.

MRS. DEARTH.   Will, try to remember this.   Did he ask us for any particular time ?

DEARTH.   Yes.   (*To above the chair* L. *of the table.*)   He was particular about its being Midsummer week.

MRS. DEARTH.   Ah !   I thought so.   Did he say what it was about me that made him want to have me here in Midsummer week ?

DEARTH.   No, but I presumed it must be your fascination.

MRS. DEARTH.   Nonsense !   Well, I want you to come out with us to-night and watch him.

DEARTH.   Spy on my host !   And such a harmless little chap, too !   Excuse me, Alice.   Besides, I have—an engagement !

MRS. DEARTH.   An engagement—with the port decanter, I presume.

DEARTH (*moving back to above the table,* C.).   A good guess, but wrong.   The decanter is now but an empty shell.   Still, how you know me !   My engagement is with a quiet cigar in the garden.

MRS. DEARTH.   Your hand is so unsteady, you won't be able to light the match.

DEARTH.   I shall just manage.

MRS. DEARTH.   A nice hand for an artist !

DEARTH.   One would scarcely call me an artist nowadays.

MRS. DEARTH.   Not so far as any work is concerned.

DEARTH (*moving a little up* L.).   Not so far as having any more pretty dreams to paint is concerned.   (*A pause as he comes down* L.C.)   Wonder why I've become such a waster, Alice ?   (*He sits* L. *of the table.*)

MRS. DEARTH.   I suppose it was always in you !

DEARTH.   I suppose so, and yet I was rather a good sort in the days when I went courting you.

MRS. DEARTH.   Yes, I thought so.   Unlucky days for me, as it has turned out.

Dearth (*quite sincere*). Yes, a bad job for you. I didn't know I was a wrong 'un at the time. Thought quite well of myself. Thought a vast deal more of you. How I used to leap out of bed at 6 a.m. all agog to be at my easel. Blood ran through my veins in those days. And now I'm middle-aged and done for—funny! Don't know how it has come about, nor what has made the music mute. (*A slight pause.*) When did you begin to despise me, Alice?

Mrs. Dearth. When I got to know you really, Will—a long time ago.

Dearth. Yes, I think that's true. It was a long time ago, and before I had begun to despise myself. It wasn't till I knew you had no opinion of me that I began to go downhill. You'll grant that, won't you?—and that I did try for a bit to fight on. If you had cared for me I wouldn't have come to this, surely?

Mrs. Dearth. Well, I found I didn't care for you, and I wasn't hypocrite enough to pretend I did. That's blunt, but you used to admire my bluntness.

Dearth. The bluntness of you—the adorable wildness of you, you untamed thing. (*He pauses, remembering.*) There were never any shades in you. You could only love or hate. Kiss or kill was your motto, Alice. I felt from the first moment I saw you that you would either love me or knife me.

Mrs. Dearth. I didn't knife you!

Dearth. No, I suppose that was where you made the mistake. It's hard on you, old lady. I suppose it's too late to try to patch things up, Alice?

Mrs. Dearth. Let's be honest. It's too late, Will.

Dearth. Perhaps if we had had children! (*He pauses.*) Pity!

Mrs. Dearth. A blessing, I should think, seeing what sort of a father they would have had!

Dearth. I daresay you're right. (*He rises, and moves round above the table.*) Well, Alice, I know that somehow it's my fault. I'm sorry for you.

Mrs. Dearth. I'm sorry for myself. If I hadn't married you, what a different woman I should be! What a fool I was!

Dearth. Ah! Three things, they say, come not back to man nor woman—the spoken word, the past life and the neglected opportunity. Wonder if we should make any more of them, Alice, if they did come back to us.

Mrs. Dearth. You wouldn't.

Dearth. I guess you're right.

Mrs. Dearth. But I——

Dearth (*coming down above her chair*). Yes, I daresay it would have been a boon for you, but I hope it's not "The Honourable Freddy Finch-Fallowe" you would put in my place. I know he is following you about again.

MRS. DEARTH. He followed me about, as you put it, before I knew you. I don't know why I quarrelled with him.

DEARTH. Your heart told you that he was no good.

MRS. DEARTH. My heart told me that you were. So it wasn't of much service to me, my heart !

DEARTH. Freddy Finch-Fallowe is a rotter, Alice.

MRS. DEARTH. You are certainly an authority on the subject.

DEARTH. You have me there. Poor old Alice. After which brief, but pleasant little connubial chat he pursued his dishonoured way into the garden.

(DEARTH *crosses up towards the windows. But he is prevented doing so by the arrival of all the others.* PURDIE *enters from the dining-room, others from* L. *headed by* LOB, *attired for the walk. Cries of* " Here we are ! " " I'm quite excited ! " " Mr. Coade, you lead the way ! " *The idea is that they are going off by the door* L. MRS. DEARTH *rises, and turns* R. *to the settee.*)

LOB (*excited—to* MR. *and* MRS. DEARTH *and* PURDIE). Come on, come on !

MRS. COADE. Are you not coming, Mr. Dearth ?

DEARTH. Alas ! Unavoidably detained. You'll find me in the garden when you come back.

JOANNA (*humorously*). If we ever do come back !

DEARTH. Precisely ! (*To his wife.*) Should we never meet again, Alice, fare thee well. Purdie, if you find the tree of knowledge in the wood, bring me back an apple.

PURDIE. I promise. (*He crosses* L. *to the door, and is checked by* LOB.)

LOB (*on needles*). Don't speak so loud. Matey might hear you.

LADY CAROLINE (*up* L.C. *Always ready to pounce on him*). Matey ! That man again ! What difference would that make, Lob ?

LOB. He would take me off to bed. It's past my time.

(*All are amused.*)

COADE. You know, old fellow, you make it very difficult for us to embark upon this adventure in the proper eerie spirit. (*A movement to go.*)

DEARTH (*turning up* C.). I'm for the garden.

(DEARTH *goes to the window, is pulling aside the curtain when he turns back. Something he has seen has startled him, though this must not be too greatly emphasised. He looks at the others, comes in and places his cigar on the ashtray up* R.)

PURDIE. How now, Dearth ?

DEARTH (*who has turned very quiet—coming down to the table,* C.). What is it we get in that wood, Lob ?

MRS. DEARTH. Ah, he won't tell us that.
LOB (*trying to get them to door* L.). Come on!
MRS. DEARTH. Tell us first.

(*They all look at* LOB. *A pause. All are silent and still.*)

LOB (*compelled to tell*). They say—that in the wood—you
get what nearly everybody here is longing for—a second chance.
(*He moves softly to the chair* L. *of the table, and sits.*)

(*A slight pause, as the ladies exchange glances.*)

JOANNA (*to* L. *of the chair above the table*). So that's what we
have in common!
ALL (*softly, looking at each other*). Ah!
COADE (L.C., *to* MRS. COADE). You know, I've often thought,
Coady, that if I had a second chance, I could be a useful man
instead of just a lazy one.
MRS. DEARTH. A second chance!
PURDIE. A second chance!
LOB (*rising*). Come on! (*Endeavouring to push them all
towards the door* L.)

(*A general movement towards* L.)

DEARTH (*still quiet*). Stop! (*They all check, and face him.*)
Why not go this way?

(DEARTH'S *manner has not been such as to rouse any suspicion in
the audience. He pulls the window curtains and, instead of a
garden, we now see close up to window and extending into the
far distance a wood of great beech trees. It is very mysterious,
with black splashes relieved by streaks of moonlight. Everybody
is startled, most of all* LOB, *on whom all eyes gradually turn.*)

LOB (*in terror*). Matey! Call Matey! (*He sits* L. *of the table,
staring at the windows.*)

(NOTE.—MRS. DEARTH *has risen. The other ladies take one step
to the men for protection, but it should be still eerie, not funny.*)

DEARTH (*up* C.). Anyone ready to risk it?

(*There is silence.*)

PURDIE (*coming forward to up* L.C.). Of course there's nothing
in it—just—er—just——
DEARTH. Of course. Going out, Purdie?

(PURDIE *shrinks back—silence.*)

MRS. DEARTH (*after the pause*). A second chance. (*Facing*
DEARTH *across the table.*)
DEARTH. I'll be back in a moment—probably.

(DEARTH *goes out and is lost in the wood. As he steps into it he puts his hands to his ears as if something strange came over him at that moment.*
The others look at one another. There is another pause.)

LADY CAROLINE. He doesn't come back. (*She crosses to* R. *of the windows.*)

MRS. COADE. It's horrible! I'm going to my room. (*To* COADE.) Come, dear.

(MRS. COADE *exits* L.)

COADE. Yes, yes.

(COADE *takes a step after her, then comes back, to* L.C.)

(*Suddenly,* MRS. PURDIE *crosses up* C., *walks out of the window, and is lost.*

NOTE.—*She does the same business with her hands and ears as* DEARTH *had done, and this is repeated by all who go into the wood.*)

PURDIE (*taking a step after her*). Mabel!

MRS. DEARTH. You'll have to go now, Mr. Purdie.

(PURDIE *moves up to the windows slowly.* JOANNA *crosses to him. He looks at* JOANNA *and they go out together.*)

LOB (*imploringly*). That's enough. Don't you go, Mrs. Dearth. Stay with me. You'll catch it if you go.

MRS. DEARTH (*moving up* C.). A second chance!

(MRS. DEARTH *walks out into the wood.*)

LADY CAROLINE (*moving up to the window. Slowly*). One— would like—to know.

(LADY CAROLINE *follows* MRS. DEARTH.)

MRS. COADE (*calling from off* L.). Coady!

(COADE *hesitates between the door and the window. Then he tiptoes up* C., *and exits into the wood.*
LOB *rises slowly and back a pace or two to* L.C.
MATEY *enters, up* R., *from the dining-room with a tray with coffee and cake. He does not see the window.*)

MATEY (*coming to above the chair* R. *of the table*). It's past your bedtime, sir. (*Putting down the tray.*) Say good night to the ladies and come along.

LOB (*pointing up* C.). Matey—look!

(MATEY *wheels round and looks at the windows. He is speechless. Then he turns to face down, slowly, and they look at each other, quaking.*)

MATEY. Great Heavens ! It's true, then !

LOB. Yes, but I—I wasn't sure !

MATEY, *shuddering, goes up to the windows to peer, but not to go out. He is backing a pace down, when* LOB, *who has gone up behind him, pushes him out.* MATEY *disappears into the wood, putting up his hands as the others have done.*

LOB *is terrified still, and backs to* L. *of the windows—yet he gloats, also. He stretches his hand to the switch and turns out the lights, and stands, with his back to the audience, silhouetted against the moonlight, as—*

The CURTAIN *falls.*

ACT II

SCENE.—*The Wood.*

The scene is the wood, in the glory of a moonlight night. It is the same scene as the wood we saw from the windows, but now we have its full depth and wealth of trees.

(See the Ground Plan at the end of the book.)

The ground is mossy and leaf-strewn, and there are small twigs and branches here and there.

When the CURTAIN *rises, the stage is almost dark and the moonlight fades in slowly.*

Bright, strange music is heard at the beginning suggesting the " Light that never was on sea or shore." The nightingale is heard and continues singing until the lights are full up. Until then there is no talk.

Seated together on the sward a little R. *of* C., *are a pair whom we have known in different conditions. We don't yet see who the man is ; he is lying on his back with a handkerchief over his face and his head on the lady's lap. He is dressed in a motor-coat, rather loudly, in the manner of an affluent City man. The lady is* LADY CAROLINE LANEY, *in an elegant country attire, suggestive of motoring. Her manner is quite changed. She neither drawls her words nor calls herself a person. She is rather jolly. We are to discover that the second chance has converted these two into man and wife.*

There is a long pause before speaking as the lights are brought up.

LADY CAROLINE (*sentimental and very unlike her old self*). Isn't it a lovely night, Jim ? Listen to Philomel.

(The nightingale is heard again. LADY CAROLINE *imitates its note sentimentally.)*

It's saying it is lately married. (*To the unseen bird.*) So are we, you ducky thing ! (*To her husband.*) I feel, Jim, that I am Rosalind, and that you are my Orlando.

MATEY (*sitting up and leaning on his elbow and disclosing himself—taking handkerchief off his face*). What do you say I am, Caroliney ?

LADY CAROLINE. My own one, don't you think it would be fun if we were to write poems about each other and pin them on the tree-trunks ?

MATEY (*tolerantly*). Poems ! I never knew such a lass for high-flown language.

LADY CAROLINE. Your lass, dearest—Jim's lass !

MATEY. And don't you forget it !

28

LADY CAROLINE. What would you do if I were to forget it, great bear ? (*Archly.*)

MATEY. Take a stick to you.

LADY CAROLINE. I love to hear you talk like that. It's so virile. I always knew that it was a *master* I needed.

MATEY. It's what you all need.

LADY CAROLINE. It is—it is ! You knowing wretch !

MATEY. Listen, Caroliney ! (*He rattles his pocket.*) That's what gets the ladies.

LADY CAROLINE. How much have you made this week, you wonderful man ?

MATEY (*blandly*). Another five hundred or so. (*Getting out a cigar.*) That's all—just five hundred or so.

LADY CAROLINE. My dear golden fetter, listen to him ! (*Looking at her wedding ring.*) Kiss my fetter, Jim.

MATEY (*bus. with matches*). Wait till I light this.

LADY CAROLINE. Let me light the darling match. (*She daintily does so while he continues.*)

MATEY. Tidy-looking Petitey Corona this ! There was a time when one of that sort would have run away with two days of my screw !

LADY CAROLINE. How I should have loved, Jim, to know you when you were poor ! Fancy your having once been a clerk !

MATEY. We all have our beginning. (*Puffing his cigar.*) But it wouldn't have mattered how I began, Caroliney. I would have come to the top just the same. (*Proudly.*) I am a climber, and there's nails in my boots for the parties beneath me. Boots ! I tell you if I had been a bootmaker, I would have been the first bootmaker in London.

LADY CAROLINE (*archly*). I'm sure you would, Jim ; but would you have made the best boots ?

MATEY (*as if she had paid him a compliment*). Ha, ha ! Very good, Caroliney ; that's the neatest thing I've heard you say. But it's late. We had best be strolling back to our Rolls.

LADY CAROLINE (*she rises and helps him up*). I do hope the ground wasn't damp ! (*Her hand on his arm.*)

MATEY. Don't matter if it was. I was lying on your rug.

(LADY CAROLINE, *however, has been on the bare ground. She picks up the rug.* JOANNA *comes on* R. *in a country dress which should suggest that she is miserable ; she is no longer the jolly, high-spirited girl we have known, but sad and crushed. They don't know each other. She passes to* L. *in front of them.*)

Who's the mournful party ?

JOANNA (*turning at* R. *of the* L. *lower tree*). I wonder, sir, whether you happen to have seen my husband ? I have lost him in the wood. (*She is sobbing.*)

(*Gay woodland music is heard softly off stage.*)

MATEY (*at* C.). We are strangers in these parts ourselves, missis. Have we passed anyone, Caroliney ?

LADY CAROLINE (R.C., *coyly*). Should we have noticed, dear ? Might it be the old gent over there ? (*Looking* R.)

(*The music is nearer.*)

MATEY (*to* JOANNA, *who has moved up* L.C.). Is that him ?

JOANNA. Oh, no ! My husband is quite young.

(COADE, *fancifully attired in a light summer suit and panama, is passing along happily at the back, playing on a whistle he has cut from a twig, and dancing to it as he goes. They survey* COADE *as he frisks along* R. *to* L.)

MATEY. Seems a merry old cock ! (*Calling.*) Hi, sir !

(COADE *comes back from up* L., *to down* L.C.)

Evening to you, sir. Do you happen to have seen a young gentleman in the wood lately, all by himself, and looking for his wife ?

(NOTE.—COADE *only seems to be playing. The music is really from an oboe off stage and ceases when* COADE *speaks. The special gramophone record should be used if possible.*)

COADE (L.C.). Can't say I have.

JOANNA (*faltering*). He isn't necessarily by himself—and I don't know that he's looking for me. There may be a—a young lady with him.

LADY CAROLINE. Oho !

JOANNA (*flashing and nearly blubbering*). What do you mean by " Oho " ?

LADY CAROLINE. Pooh ! If you like that better.

MATEY. Now, now, now—your manners, Caroliney.

COADE. Would he be singing or dancing ?

JOANNA. Oh, no !—at least, I hope not.

COADE (*to whom this is a strange hope*). Hope not ? Odd ! Then I'm not likely to notice him. But if I do—what name shall I say ?

JOANNA. Purdie. I am Mrs. Purdie.

COADE. I'll try to keep a look out, and if I see him . . . But I am rather occupied at present.

(COADE *dances a whimsical sword dance over his whistle and another stick crossed, and then goes off up* L., *playing and dancing.*)

JOANNA (*to* MATEY). I'm sorry I troubled you. I see him now. (*Looking* R. *up stage*.)

LADY CAROLINE (*without looking*). Is he alone ?

(JOANNA *glares at her*.)

Ah ! I see he isn't !

MATEY. Caroliney, no awkward questions ! (*Moving up stage*.) Evening, missis, and I hope you'll get him to go along with you quietly. (*Looking after* COADE.) Look at the old codger dancing.

(CAROLINE, *behind him, looks off in the same direction. The whistle is heard in the distance. They go off, skipping like* COADE, *and singing, to* L., *up stage.*

The music ceases.

JOANNA, *the jealous, hides behind the tree down* L. *as* MR. *and* MRS. PURDIE *enter up* R. *in smart country clothes. He now thinks that* JOANNA *is his wife and* MABEL *his only love.* MABEL *is now bright and vivacious. It is as if she and* JOANNA *had changed characters. It is* MRS. PURDIE *who is the pursued now, instead of having to pursue. She banters him, which makes him hotter in the chase.*

(PURDIE *enters* R., *looks round carefully, and turns at* C.)

PURDIE (*calling*). It's all right. She's gone.

(MRS. PURDIE *comes on gaily at* R., *eludes his advance, hides behind the tree* R. *and is pursued by* PURDIE *round the tree, down, and gets to* R. *of the* R. *tree.*)

(*After the above bus.*) Now, will you ? Please do !

MRS. PURDIE (*bantering*). No, and no, and *no* ! I don't know you nearly well enough for that. Besides, what would your wife say ? I shall begin to think you are a very dreadful man, Mr. Purdie.

PURDIE (*who is as sincere as ever ; below and to* L. *of the tree*). Surely you might call me Jack by this time ?

MRS. PURDIE (*also sincere*). Only if you are very good—Jack. (*To* PURDIE.)

PURDIE. If only Joanna were more like you !

MRS. PURDIE. Like me ? You mean her face—it's a—well, if it's not precisely pretty, it's a good face. *I* don't mind her face at all. I'm glad you've got such a dependable little wife, Jack.

PURDIE (*gloomily*). Thanks ! (*He leans against the tree.*)

(MRS. PURDIE *crosses to* L. *of him and he goes to kiss her.* JOANNA *peeps at them at times and we understand her feelings from her face.*)

MRS. PURDIE (*eluding him, to* C.). . . . No, you stand over there—and behave. What would Joanna have said if she had seen you just now ? (*She reclines on the ground down* C.)

PURDIE (*on her* R., *and below her*). A wife should be incapable of jealousy.

MRS. PURDIE (*pretending innocence*). Joanna jealous ! But has she any reasons ? Jack, tell me, who is the woman ?

PURDIE. Shall I, Mabel, shall I ? (*He kneels by her*.)

MRS. PURDIE (*faltering*). I can't think who she is. Have I ever seen her ?

PURDIE (*as if it were an original remark*). Every time you look in a mirror.

MRS. PURDIE (*thoughtfully*). How odd ! Jack, that can't be. When I look in the mirror I only see myself.

PURDIE (*believing her*). How adorably innocent you are, Mabel ! Joanna would have guessed at once.

MRS. PURDIE (*startled*). Oh ! Oh ! I believe I . . . Oh, Jack.

PURDIE. Shall I tell you now ? The old, old story.

(*A little cry from* JOANNA, *behind her tree down* L.)

BOTH. What's that ?

PURDIE. It's only that robin. Shall I tell you . . . ? (*He leans a little towards her and pauses*.)

MRS. PURDIE (*faltering*). I don't know, I'm sure. Jack, try not to say it, but if you feel you must, say it in such a way that it would not hurt the feelings of Joanna if she happened to be passing by—as she nearly always is.

PURDIE. I'd rather not say it at all than that way. I don't know, Mabel, whether you have noticed that I am not like other men ?

MRS. PURDIE. Yes.

PURDIE. All my life I have been a soul that has had to walk alone.

MRS. PURDIE. How tragic !

PURDIE. I do so still. Then I met Joanna——

(JOANNA *sniffs—he looks up*.)

MRS. PURDIE. Ah !

PURDIE. Foolishly, as I now see, I thought she would understand that I was far too deep a nature really to mean the little things I sometimes said to her.

MRS. PURDIE. And so you married her.

PURDIE. And so I married her. (*A sob from* JOANNA.) But still my soul walked alone.

MRS. PURDIE. Then you met me ?

PURDIE. Then—I met you. (*He draws a little closer*.)

MRS. PURDIE. Too late—never—for ever—for ever—never ! They are the saddest words in the English tongue.

PURDIE. At the time I thought a still sadder word
Joanna——

MRS. PURDIE. What was it you saw in me that made you
love me ?

PURDIE (*his arms round her*). I think it was the feeling that
you were so like myself.

(PURDIE *murmurs something to himself. She draws away from
him.*)

MRS. PURDIE. You are saying something to yourself, Jack.
What is it ? Don't keep anything from me.

PURDIE (*fervently*). I was repeating a poem, dear. It is
in two words—" Mabel Purdie."

MRS. PURDIE. Oh !

PURDIE (*kneeling*). Mabel Purdie ! If it could only be !
Say " Mabel Purdie " to me. Say it once, dear.

MRS. PURDIE. If I were to say it, Jack. (*She is practically
in his arms now.*) I should be false to Joanna——

(*They embrace.*)

And that I swear I shall never be.

PURDIE (*rising*). Mabel !

MRS. PURDIE. Let us go on. (*She rises.*)

PURDIE. Say it, Mabel, say it !

MRS. PURDIE. I'll whisper it. (*She does so.*)

(*The nightingale is heard again.* PURDIE *and* MRS. PURDIE *move
up, his arm round her waist, and off up* L. JOANNA, *bedraggled
and miserable, moves up* C. *and turns. Before following them
off, she looks up at the tree* R., *and addresses the unseen bird.*)

JOANNA. That's all you know—you *bird !*

(JOANNA *turns and exits up* L.)

(*But the nightingale is really singing for another pair he has espied
below. Apparently they are racing to the spot, and there is a
prize for the one who finds where the easel was put up last night.
The winner is* MARGARET, *who enters* R., *a boyish figure of
a girl not yet grown to womanhood. Brambles adhere to her
dress. One boot has been in the water. Her hair is short and
unruly, and she has many freckles. Yet she is as lovely as you
think she is, and she is aged the moment when you like your
daughter best.
A hoot of triumph from her brings her father to the spot. We
have already heard him as he approached, singing a song picked
up in the Latin Quarter.*)

MARGARET (*calling to him off* R.). Daddy—Daddy ! I've
won ! Here's the place ! Crack-in-my-eye, Tommy !

(*Her father enters. It is* DEARTH. *But he is now an engaging fellow in tweeds, ablaze in happiness and health, and carrying easel and paint-box. He looks around, and nods approvingly, setting his easel up at* L.C. *as he speaks.*)

DEARTH. Yes, that's the tree I stuck my easel under last night, (*in burlesque, pointing to the sky*) and behold the blessèd moon behaving more gorgeously than ever. I'm sorry to have kept you waiting, old lady, but you ought to know by now how time passes. (*Setting out his materials*') Now, keep still, while I hand you down to posterity.

(NOTE.—*The moon is supposed to be down stage* R., *not visible to the audience.*)

MARGARET (C., R. *of* DEARTH). She's rather pale to-night, isn't she ?

(MARGARET *puts her cap in his pocket. Now and again throughout the scene she makes use of his pockets as receptacles for her various articles.*)

DEARTH. Comes of keeping late hours.

MARGARET (*to the moon, gaily coming down a little*). Daddy, watch me—look at me ! (*To the moon.*) Please, sweet moon, a pleasant expression—No, no—not as if you were sitting for it—that's too professional. That's better. (*She drops the moon a curtsy.*) Thank you. Now keep it. (*Turning up to* DEARTH.) That's the sort of thing you say to them, Dad !

DEARTH (*getting to work*). You're a monkey ! You know I oughtn't to have brought you out so late. You should be tucked up in your cosy bed at home.

MARGARET. With the pillows, anyhow. (*Throwing beech nuts off* L.)

DEARTH. Except in its proper place !

MARGARET. And the sheet over my face. (*A pace or two towards* R.C.)

DEARTH. Where it oughtn't to be.

MARGARET (*turning to face* DEARTH). And daddy tiptoeing in to take it off.

DEARTH. Which is more than you deserve.

MARGARET (*a pace to* C.). Then why does he stand so long at the door ? And before he's gone she bursts out laughing, for she has been awake all the time. (*Back of him.*)

(*She is now above him, glancing at the picture.*)

DEARTH. That's about it ! What a life. But I oughtn't to have brought you here. Best to have the sheet over you when the moon's about. Moonlight's bad for little daughters.

MARGARET. Daddy . . . (*To* C.) I can't sleep when the

moon's at the full.   She keeps calling to me to get up.   Perhaps
I'm *her* daughter too.

DEARTH.   Gad, you look it to-night !

MARGARET (*pleased*).   Do I ?   Then can't you paint me into
the picture as well as Mamma ?   You could call it " A mother
and daughter," or simply, " Two ladies," if the moon thinks that
calling me her daughter would make her seem too old.

DEARTH.   O mater pulchra filia pulchrior !   That means, " O
Moon—more beautiful than any twopenny-ha'penny daughter " !

MARGARET (*mischievously, pouting*).   Daddy, do you really
prefer her ?

(*To him, he kisses her lightly.*)

DEARTH (*in stage whisper*).   H'sh !   She's not a patch on you.
It's the sort of thing we say to our sitters to keep them in good
humour. (*Struck by something on her frock.*)   Come here.
(*Examines it—evidently it is a stain.   He sighs.*)   I wish to
heaven, Margaret, you and I weren't both so fond of apple
tart !   (*Catching hold of her skirt.*)   And what's this ?

MARGARET.   It's a tear !

DEARTH.   I should think it is a tear !

MARGARET (*sliding a little R. and turning*).   It was that boy
at the farm.   He kept calling Snubs after me, but I got him
down and kicked him in the stomach.   He's rather a jolly boy.
(*She goes up, above and to R. of* DEARTH.)

DEARTH.   Ye gods !   What a night !

MARGARET (*looking at his picture*).   And what a moon !   Dad,
she's not quite so fine as that.

DEARTH.   'Sh !   I've touched her up !

(COADES'S *music is heard again.   He dances in up* L., *and across
up stage to* R.)

MARGARET (*as* COADE *reaches* C.).   Dad, Dad—what a funny
man !

(MARGARET *gaily dances behind* COADE, *imitating him.   He disappears up* R., *but his whistling is still heard.*   DEARTH *joins*
MARGARET *in a wild dance.   She ends in his arms, at* C., *suddenly sad and fearful.*)

Hold me tight, Daddy, I'm frightened.   I think they want to
take you away from me.

DEARTH.   Who, gosling ?

MARGARET.   I don't know.   It's too lovely, Daddy.   I won't
be able to keep hold of it.

DEARTH.   What is ?

MARGARET.   The world—everything—and you, Daddy, most
of all.   Things that are too beautiful can't last.

DEARTH (*who knows it*).   Now, how did you find that out ?

MARGARET (*still in his arms*). I don't know, Daddy. Am I sometimes stranger than other people's daughters ?

DEARTH. More of a mad-cap, perhaps.

(*He kisses her.*)

MARGARET. Do you think I am sometimes *too* full of gladness ?

DEARTH. You are sometimes running over with it. (*He goes to the easel.*)

MARGARET. To be very gay, dearest dear, is so near to being very sad.

DEARTH (*who knows this, also*). How did you find that out, child ?

MARGARET. I don't know. From something in me that's afraid. (*She sits on the ground* C.) Daddy, what is a " might-have-been " ?

DEARTH (*to easel*). A " might-have-been " ? They're ghosts, Margaret ! I daresay I " might-have-been " a great swell of a painter, instead of just this uncommonly happy nobody—or again I might have been a worthless idle waster of a fellow.

MARGARET (*incredulous, sitting up*). You ?

DEARTH. Who knows ? Some little kink in me might have set me off on the wrong road. And that poor soul I might so easily have been might have had no Margaret. I'm sorry for *him*. (*He sits at the easel.*)

MARGARET (*sitting back*). And so am I ! (*Playing with twigs.*) The poor old daddy, wandering about the world without me.

DEARTH. And there are other " might-have-beens "—lovely ones, but intangible. *Shades*, Margaret, made of sad folks' thoughts.

MARGARET (*gaily*). I'm so glad I'm not a shade. How awful it would be, Daddy, to wake up and find one wasn't alive.

DEARTH. It would, dear.

MARGARET. Daddy, wouldn't it be awful ? (*A slight pause.*) I think men need daughters.

DEARTH. They do.

MARGARET. Especially artists.

DEARTH. Especially artists.

MARGARET. Especially artists.

DEARTH. Especially artists.

MARGARET. Fame is not everything.

DEARTH (*in same spirit*). Fame is rot ! Daughters are the thing !

MARGARET. Daughters are the thing.

DEARTH. Daughters are the thing.

MARGARET. I wonder if sons would be even nicer ?

DEARTH. Not a patch on daughters. The awful thing about a son is that never—never—at least, from the day he goes to school—can you tell him that you rather like him. By the time

he's ten you can't even take him on your knee. Sons are not
worth having, Margaret. Signed, W. Dearth.
    MARGARET (*still on the ground*). But if you were a mother,
Dad, I daresay he would let you do it.
    DEARTH. Think so ?
    MARGARET. I mean, when no one was looking. Sons are
not so bad. Signed M. Dearth. But I'm glad you prefer
daughters. (*Coming to him on her knees.*) At what age are we
nicest, Daddy ? (*But he is engrossed in his moon.*) Hie, Daddy,
at what age are we nicest ? (*He seems not to hear.*) Daddy—
hie ! Hie—at what age are we nicest ?
    DEARTH (*rising*). Eh ? (*Jocular and tender at the same time.*)
That's a poser ! I think you were nicest when you were two
and knew your alphabet up to " G " but fell over at " H."
(*He paints a stroke or two.*) No, you were best when you were
half past three—or just before you struck six—or in the mumps
year, when I asked you in the early morning how you were and
you said solemnly, " I haven't tried yet." (*He moves back a
pace, viewing the picture.*) I'm not sure that chicken-pox doesn't
beat mumps. (*Down* L.C. *and turns.*) Oh, Lord ! I'm all
wrong. The nicest time in a father's life is *now,* the year before
she puts up her hair.
    MARGARET. (*thoughtfully*). I suppose that is a splendid time
for fathers. But there's a nicer year coming to you, Daddy,
the year she *does* put up her hair.
    DEARTH. Suddenly puts it up for ever ? You know, I am
afraid that when the day for that comes I won't be able to
stand it, it will be too exciting. My poor heart, Margaret !
    MARGARET (*still on the ground*). No, no, it will be *lucky* you,
for it isn't to be a bit like that. I'm to be a girl and woman
day about, for the first year. You'll never know which I am
till you look at my hair. And even then you won't know, for
if it's down I'll put it up, and if it's up I'll put it down. (*Import-
antly.*) And, so my daddy will gradually get used to the idea.
(*She rises.*)
    DEARTH. I see you have been thinking it out. (*He moves
up to the easel again.*)
    MARGARET. I have been doing more than that. Shut your
eyes, Daddy, and I'll give you a glimpse into the future.
    DEARTH. I don't know that I want that. The present's so
good.
    MARGARET. Shut your eyes at once.
    DEARTH. No, Margaret.
    MARGARET. Please, Daddy.
    DEARTH. Oh, all right. (*Doing so.*) They are shut !
    MARGARET. Don't open them till I tell you. What finger is
that ? (*Holding up a thumb.*)
    DEARTH. The dirty one.

(DEARTH *hums a French song. She begins to put up her hair, using as mirror a little pool of water on the ground,* L. *of the middle tree at* R.)

MARGARET (*kneeling by the pool*). Daddy, now I am putting up my hair. I have got such a darling of a mirror. It's such a darling mirror I've got, Dad. Dad, don't look. It's such a darling mirror. I'll tell you about it. It's a little pool of water. I wish we could take it home and hang it up. Of course the moment my hair is up there will be other changes also. For one thing, I shall talk quite differently.

DEARTH. Pooh ! Where are my matches, dear ? (*Feeling his pockets with his eyes shut.*)

MARGARET. Top pocket, waistcoat.

DEARTH (*trying to light his pipe, eyes closed*). You were trying to frighten me just now.

MARGARET (*still kneeling at the pool*). No, I am just preparing you. You see, darling, I can't call you Daddy when my hair is up. I think I shall call you—(*reflects*) I shall call you—parent. Parent dear, do you remember the days when your Margaret was a slip of a girl, and sat on your knee ? How foolish we were, Parent, in those distant days !

DEARTH. Shut up, Margaret.

MARGARET. Now I must be more distant to you—more like the boy who couldn't sit on your knee any more.

DEARTH. See here, I want to go on painting. Shall I look now ?

MARGARET (*rather quaking now*). No—no—no—— (*She looks in pool.*) I am not quite sure whether I want you to. It makes such a difference. Perhaps you won't know me. Even the pool is looking a little scared. (*She comes* C., *anxiously.*) Look, Daddy. What do you think ? Will I do ?

DEARTH. Stand still, dear, and let me look my fill. (*He looks long at her.*) The Margaret that is to be.

MARGARET. You'll see me often enough, Daddy, like this, so you don't need to look your fill. You are looking as long as if this were to be the only time.

DEARTH. Was I ? Surely it can't be that ?

MARGARET. Be gay, Dad. (*She moves to him, and puts her arms round him.*) You will be sick of Margaret with her hair up before you are done with her.

DEARTH. I expect so.

MARGARET. Shut up, Daddy ! (*She moves a little* R., *letting her hair down.*) Daddy, I know what you are thinking of. You are thinking what a handful she is going to be.

DEARTH (*humorously*). Well, I guess she is !

MARGARET (*grave*). Daddy, now you are thinking about—about my being in love some day.

DEARTH. Rot!

MARGARET (*reassuringly*). I won't, you know, no, never! (*Coming nearer to him.*) Oh, I've quite decided, so don't be afraid, Daddy. (*At back of him* L.C.,—*whispers.*) Will you hate him at first, Daddy?

DEARTH. Whom?

(*During the following lines,* DEARTH *paints assiduously.*)

MARGARET. Well, if there was!

DEARTH. If there was what, darling?

MARGARET. You know the kind of thing I mean, quite well. Would you hate him at first?

DEARTH. I hope not. I should want to strangle him, but I wouldn't hate him.

MARGARET. *I* would. (*Moving to* C.) That is to say, if I liked him.

DEARTH. If you liked him, how could you hate him?

MARGARET (*up* C.). For daring!

DEARTH. Daring what?

MARGARET. You know! (*Sighing half-humorously.*) But of course *I* shall have no say in the matter.

DEARTH. Why?

MARGARET (*reproachfully*). *You* will do it all. You do everything for me.

DEARTH (*with a groan*). I can't help it.

MARGARET (*sauntering to* L.C., *kicking twigs and leaves*). You will even write my love-letters, if I ever have any to write— which I won't.

DEARTH (*properly alarmed*). Surely to goodness I'll leave you alone to do that!

MARGARET (*standing by the tree, behind the easel*). Not you. You'll try to, but you won't be able.

(DEARTH *stops painting.*)

DEARTH. I want you, you see, to do everything exquisitely. (*Remorseful.*) I wish I could leave you to do things a little more for yourself. (*As he paints a few strokes.*) I suppose it's owing to my having to be father and mother both. I knew nothing practically about the rearing of children—and of course I couldn't trust you to a nurse.

MARGARET (*severely—crossing down* C., *below and* R. *of the easel*). Not you. So sure you could do it better yourself. That's you all over. (*Turning, and shaking her head solemnly at him.*) Of course I know you can't help it. (*Moving up* C. *to* R. *of* DEARTH.) If I ever *should* marry—not that I will —but if I should—will you let *me* be the one who says " I do "?

DEARTH (*groaning*). I suppose I deserve this !

MARGARET (*sitting* O.). Daddy, do you remember how you taught me to balance a biscuit on my nose, like a puppy ?

DEARTH (*sadly*). Did I ?

MARGARET. And when you said " snap " I caught it in my mouth ?

DEARTH. Horrible !

MARGARET (*kneeling up, and whispering*). Daddy ! I can do it still. (*Producing a biscuit.*) Here is the last of my supper. (*She puts it on her nose.*) Say " snap," Daddy.

DEARTH. Not I.

MARGARET. Say snap, please.

DEARTH. No, Margaret.

MARGARET. Daddy !

DEARTH. Snap !

(MARGARET *catches the biscuit in her mouth.*)

Let that be the last time, Margaret. (*He resumes his painting.*)

MARGARET. Except just once more.

DEARTH (*putting down his brush*). No, darling.

MARGARET (*sitting back*). Not now. (*Wheedling and shy.*) But if I should ever have a—a Margaret of my own, come in and see me, Daddy, in my bed, and say " snap "—and I'll have the biscuit ready.

DEARTH (*turning away his head*). Right-o.

MARGARET. *You* think I'm pretty, don't you, Daddy, whatever other people say ? (*Sitting by him.*)

DEARTH (*taking up his brush*). Not so bad.

MARGARET. I *know* I have nice ears.

DEARTH (*painting*). They are all right now, but I had to work on them for months.

MARGARET. You don't mean to say that you did my *ears* ?

DEARTH. Rather !

MARGARET (*entreating*). My dimple's my own, isn't it ?

DEARTH (*drawing back and regarding the painting*). I'm glad you think so. I wore out the point of my little finger over that dimple.

MARGARET. Even my dimple ! Have I anything that's really mine ? A bit of my nose or anything ?

DEARTH (*sighing*). When you were a babe you had a laugh that was all your own.

MARGARET. Haven't I it now ?

DEARTH. It's gone. (*He is a good deal moved, and rises, moving up* O.,—*sadly*). I'll tell you how it went. We were fishing in a stream—that is to say, I was wading and you were sitting on my shoulders doing the fishing. We didn't catch anything. Somehow or another—I can't think how I did it— you irritated me, and I answered you sharply. (*He shudders.*)

MARGARET (*who is on ground* c. *below him*). I can't believe that.

DEARTH (*behind her, moving about*). Yes, I did. It gave you a shock, and, for the moment, the world no longer seemed a safe place to you. Your faith in me had always made it safe till then. You were suddenly not even sure of your bread and butter, and a frightened tear came to your eyes. I was in a nice state, I can tell you. (*He looks down at her.*)

MARGARET (*looking up at him*). But what has that to do with my laugh, Daddy ?

DEARTH. The laugh that children are born with lasts just so long as they have perfect faith. To think it was I who robbed you of yours. I expect I am not the only parent in that plight, though they may not remember the doing of it. (*He is crushed.*)

MARGARET. Don't, dear ! I'm sure the laugh just went off with the tear to comfort it, and they have been playing about that stream ever since. They have quite forgotten us, so why should we remember them ? Shall I tell you my farthest-back recollection ?

(*He nods—and strolls to down* R.C.)

(*She speaks in some awe.*) I remember the first time I saw the stars.

(*He nods again.*)

I had never seen the *night*, and then I saw *it*, and the *stars*, together. Crack-in-my-eye, Tommy !—not everyone can boast of such a lovely recollection for their earliest !

DEARTH. I was determined your earliest should be a good one.

MARGARET. Do you mean to say *you* planned it.

DEARTH (*to her—at* C.). Rather ! Most people's earliest recollection is of some trivial thing ; how they cut their finger or lost a piece of string. I was resolved my Margaret's should be something bigger. I was poor, but I could give her the stars.

MARGARET (*impulsively, she clasps his knee*). Oh, how you do love me, Daddy !

DEARTH. Yes, I do rather.

(*It is the climax of their scene of affection.* MARGARET *releases* DEARTH, *and he returns to his easel.*

MRS. DEARTH *enters down* R. *She is poor in dress and worn in appearance, but with the simpering airs and touches of the fine lady—though she is almost a vagrant. They do not know each other.*)

MARGARET (*nicely*). Good evening.

MRS. DEARTH. Good evening, missy. Evening, mister. (*She is looking about among the roots of the trees.*)

DEARTH (*at the easel—at work*). Lost anything ?

MRS. DEARTH. Sometimes when the tourists have had their sandwiches there's bits left over, and they squeeze them between the roots to keep the place tidy. I'm looking for bits.

DEARTH. You don't tell me you are as hungry as all that ?

MRS. DEARTH. Try me.

MARGARET (*feeling his pocket*). Daddy, that was my last biscuit !

DEARTH. We must think of something else.

MARGARET (*up* L. *to* MRS. DEARTH). Wait a bit, we're sure to think of something. Daddy, think of something. (*She puts her hand on* MRS. DEARTH'S *shoulder.*)

MRS. DEARTH. Your father doesn't like you to touch the likes of me.

MARGARET. Oh, yes, he does ! (*Smiling defiantly.*) And if he didn't, I'd do it all the same. This is a bit of *myself*, Daddy.

DEARTH. That's all *you* know.

MRS. DEARTH (*sulky*). You needn't be angry with her, mister, I'm all right.

DEARTH. I'm not angry with her. I'm very sorry for you.

MRS. DEARTH. If I had my rights, I would be as good as you—and better.

DEARTH. I daresay.

MRS. DEARTH. I've had menservants and a motor.

DEARTH. Margaret and I never rose to that.

MARGARET. I've been in a taxi several times, and Dad often gets telegrams.

DEARTH. Margaret !

MARGARET. I'm sorry I boasted.

MRS. DEARTH. That's nothing. I have a town house—at least, I had . . . At any rate, he said there was a town house.

MARGARET. Fancy his not knowing for certain.

MRS. DEARTH. The Honourable Mrs. Finch-Fallowe—that's who I am.

MARGARET. It's a lovely name.

MRS. DEARTH. Curse him !

MARGARET. Don't you like him ?

DEARTH (*to* MRS. DEARTH). We needn't go into these matters, I have nothing to do with your past. I wish we had some food.

MRS. DEARTH. You haven't a flask ?

DEARTH. No, I don't take anything myself. But let me see . . .

MARGARET (*sparkling*). I know. You said we had five pounds. (*To* MRS. DEARTH.) Would you like five pounds ?

DEARTH. Darling, don't be stupid. We haven't paid our bill at the inn.

MRS. DEARTH (*rising*). All right. I never asked you for anything.

DEARTH. Ah, don't take me up in that way. I've had my
ups and downs too. Here's ten bob, and welcome. (*He hands
a ten-shilling note to* MARGARET.)
MARGARET. And I have half a crown. (*Giving it to* MRS.
DEARTH *with the note.*) It's quite easy for us. Dad will be
getting another fiver any day. You can't think how exciting
it is when the fiver comes in. We dance, and then we run out
and buy chops.
DEARTH. Margaret!
MRS. DEARTH. It's kind of you. I'm richer this minute
than I've been for many a day.
DEARTH. It's nothing. I'm sure you'd do the same for us.
MRS. DEARTH. I wish I was as sure!
DEARTH. Of course you would. Glad to be of any help.
You get some food as quick as you can. Best of wishes and
may your luck change. (*He goes to the easel.*)
MRS. DEARTH. Same to you and may yours go on.
MARGARET (*giving her hand*). Good night.
MRS. DEARTH (*turning* MARGARET *round—and moving to* L. *of
her*). What's her name, Mister?
DEARTH. Margaret!
MRS. DEARTH (C.). Margaret—— You drew something good
out of the lucky bag when you got her, mister.
DEARTH. Yes.
MRS. DEARTH. Take care of her. They're easily lost.

(*She wanders off up* R.)

DEARTH. Poor soul! I guess she has had a rough time, and
that some man is to blame for it—partly, at any rate. That
woman rather affects me, Margaret. I don't know why.

(MARGARET *moves thoughtfully* L., *below the easel, as* DEARTH
*goes on painting, talking in his pauses in which he surveys his
work, mixes paint, etc.*)

I say, Margaret, we lucky ones, let's swear always to be kind to
people who are down on their luck and then when we're kind,
let's be a little kinder. (*He puts down his brush.*)
MARGARET (*moving up to his* L., *gleefully*). Yes, let's.
DEARTH (*taking her hand*). Margaret, always feel sorry for
the failures, the ones who are always, always failures—especially
in my sort of calling. Wouldn't it be lovely, to turn them on
the thirty-ninth year of failure into glittering successes?
MARGARET. Topping.
DEARTH. Topping.
MARGARET. Oh, topping. How could we do it, Daddy?
DEARTH (*returning to his painting*). By letter. " To poor
old Tom Broken Heart, Top Attic, Garret Chambers, S.E.
Dear Sir : His Majesty has been graciously pleased to purchase
your superb picture of Marlow Ferry."

MARGARET. "P.S.—I am sending the money in a sack so as you can hear it chink." (*She crosses to* R.C.)

DEARTH (*putting down his brush and palette*). What could we do for our friend who passed just now ? I can't get her out of my head. (*He comes to* C., *on* R. *of the easel.*)

MARGARET (*troubled*). Oh, you have made me forget ! (*Plaintively.*) Daddy, I didn't like it. (*She clings to him.*)

DEARTH. What is it now, dear ? Didn't like what ?

MARGARET (*with a little shudder*). I didn't like her saying that about your losing me.

DEARTH. I'll not lose you !

MARGARET. It would be hard for me if you lost me, but it would be worse for my daddy ! I don't know how I know that, but I do know it. What would you do without me ?

DEARTH (*almost sharply*). Don't talk like that, dear. It's wicked and stupid, and naughty. (*He relents, giving her a little hug. He is moved.*) Somehow that poor woman—I won't paint any more to-night. (*He turns to the easel and begins to pack up his things.*)

MARGARET. Let's get out of the wood. It frightens me.

DEARTH. And you loved it a moment ago. (*He goes on packing, whistling as he does so. Then, as he turns to glance up* C.) Hullo !

(*He has seen something strange. Part of a house has imperceptibly appeared in the background, a gauze effect. The curtained window of Act I is seen as from outside—the house is small and some distance away. He is only mildly surprised, thinking he has been unobservant.*)

I hadn't noticed there was a house there !

MARGARET (*Agitated, looking in the same direction*). Nor I. (*Going up to him.*) Daddy, I feel sure there wasn't a house there.

(*The moonlight commences to fade very slowly.*)

DEARTH. Goose ! It's just that we didn't look. Our old way of letting the world go hang ! So interested in ourselves. Nice behaviour for people who had been boasting about what they would do for other people ! That gives me an idea.

MARGARET (*gripping his arm*). Let's get out of the wood ! (*She draws him towards* R.C.)

DEARTH (*disengaging*). Yes, but my idea first. It is to rouse these people and get food from them for our friend.

MARGARET (*clutching his coat*). She's too far away now.

DEARTH (*drawing away*). I can overtake her in a jiffy.

(*Only a light between the chinks of the curtain can be seen now.*)

MARGARET (*in a frenzy*). Don't go into that house, Daddy !

I'm afraid of it !   I don't know why, but I'm afraid of that house !

(He waggles a reproving finger at her.)

DEARTH *(giving her three kisses)*.   There's a kiss for each moment until I come back.

(She wipes them from her face.)

Oh, naughty !   Go and stand in the corner.

(She stands against the tree down R., but stamps her foot.)

Who has got a nasty temper !

(She tries hard not to smile, but she has to, and he smiles too ; and they make comic faces at each other as they have done a thousand times before in similar circumstances.)

I shall be back before you can count a hundred.

(He turns and goes off up C. to L., humming his gay French song. The wood is now growing dark, and the trees more obscure. The nightingale is heard again, though farther off than before.

MARGARET tries dutifully to count her hundred, but her fear returns.   She runs panic-stricken up C., and then from tree to tree, calling.)

MARGARET. Daddy ! *(To up C.)* Daddy ! *(Running from L. to R.)* Daddy ! *(To down C., and backing to down R.)* Daddy, come back ! Come back, Daddy ! *(She turns L. of the lower R. tree, to face down.   There is no light but a faint moonbeam upon her face.)* I don't want to be a might-have-been !

(The moonbeam fades.)

CURTAIN.

ACT III

SCENE.—*As in Act I. The drawing-room is in darkness. The curtains are drawn across the windows. Outside, the wood has been replaced by the garden, but this too is in darkness and cannot be seen when the curtains are parted.*

LOB is asleep in the armchair up L., which is still turned to face up R., diagonally, so that only one of his legs can be seen, and no more.

There is a knocking at the window and then PURDIE and MRS. PURDIE enter as intruders. They are dressed (like those who follow) as at the end of Act I, but they still regard each other as in Act II. They do not see LOB yet, and are unaware that their clothes have changed.

PURDIE (*in the darkness*). I feel rather like a burglar. (*He gropes up L.C*)

MRS. PURDIE (*up R.C.*). It's quite creepy, sweetheart.

PURDIE. Ah! It's extraordinary how helpless one is in a dark room.

MRS. PURDIE. Yes, even if you know the room, and this one being strange to us makes it worse.

(PURDIE *knocks against some furniture.*)

PURDIE. One minute. I think I've fallen down a cellar.

MRS. PURDIE. Beloved, are you hurt?

PURDIE. How awful if Joanna were following us! Here's a switch.

(*He turns on the light and they look around.*)

Ah! A pretty room. I wonder who is the owner?

MRS. PURDIE (*suddenly, pointing to LOB*). There's a man!

PURDIE. Hello, he's asleep! (*He moves L. to LOB.*)

MRS. PURDIE (*moving to C., on R. of PURDIE*). Do you know him?

PURDIE. Never set eyes on him before. (*To LOB.*) Excuse me, sir! Hi!

(PURDIE *shakes LOB in vain, though LOB makes sufficient movement to show that he is alive.*)

Darling, how extraordinary! I suppose he is the owner.

MRS. PURDIE (*drawing PURDIE to C.*). After all, precious, have we any right to wake up a stranger, just to tell him that we are runaways hiding in his house?

PURDIE. I think he would expect it of us. (*Turning to LOB.*) Hi! (*Slight pause.*) There's no budging him.

MRS. PURDIE. Well, at any rate, we've done the civil thing.

46

(*She crosses to* R. *of the table, and looks at the tray with the coffee.*)
There have evidently been people here, but they haven't drunk
their coffee. (*Drinks.*) Ugh! Cold as a deserted egg in a
bird's nest. (*To below the chair* R. *of the table.*) Jack, if you
were a clever detective you could construct those people out of
their deserted coffee-cups. I wonder who they are, and what
has spirited them away?

PURDIE (*beautifully*). What does it matter ? (*Moving towards
her.*) There's just one cup I want to drink, and its name is
Mabel! (*He comes above and to her* R.)

MRS. PURDIE (*sitting* R. *of the table*). Dear! I suppose we
have run away. Jack—meaning it ?

PURDIE. Irrevocably! (*Passionately, he kneels* R. *of her
chair.*) Mabel, if the dog-like devotion of a lifetime . . . (*He
checks, and glances over at* LOB.) He's not shamming, is he ?

MRS. PURDIE. Shake him again.

(PURDIE *rises, goes up to* LOB, *returns, and kneels again.* LOB,
unseen by them, gives his kick in the air.)

PURDIE. If the dog-like devotion of a lifetime . . .

MRS. PURDIE. Poor little Joanna! Still, if a woman will be
a pendulum round a man's neck!

PURDIE. Do give me a chance, Mabel! If the dog-like
devotion of a lifetime . . .

(JOANNA *enters at the window up* C., *and stands a little melo-
dramatically, up* L.C.)

You know this is just a little too thick, Joanna! (*He remains
kneeling absurdly at* MABEL'S *side.*)

JOANNA. So, sweet husband, your soul is still walking alone,
is it ?

MRS. PURDIE. Joanna! How can you sneak about in this
way! Have you no pride ?

JOANNA. Please to address me as Mrs. Purdie, madam.
(*Looking at* LOB.) Who is this man ? (*She goes up to* LOB'S
chair.)

PURDIE. We don't know. There's no waking him. But you
can try if you like.

(JOANNA *shakes* LOB, *without result.*)

It's no good.

JOANNA (*moving to* L. *of the table*). You were saying something
about the devotion of a lifetime ? Please go on! (*She sits* L.
of the table.)

PURDIE (*rising diffidently*). I don't like to before you, Joanna.

JOANNA (*tossing her head*). Oh, don't mind me!

PURDIE (*moving above the table*). I should certainly like to
say it.

Mrs. Purdie (*defying* Joanna). And I shall be proud to hear it.

Purdie (*to* Joanna). I should have liked to spare you this. You wouldn't put your hands over your ears ?

Joanna. No, sir.

Mrs. Purdie. Fie, Joanna ! Surely a wife's natural delicacy . . .

Purdie. As you take it in that spirit, Joanna, I can proceed with a clear conscience. (*He returns to* R. *of* Mrs. Purdie.)

Joanna. Fox !

Mrs. Purdie. Sneak !

Purdie. " If the dog-like devotion of a lifetime . . ." (*He stops, dazed.*) I'm feeling very funny !

(*All rise.*)

Joanna. So am I. (*She turns up* L., *her hand to her forehead.*)

Mrs. Purdie (*bewildered*). I think I have been in this room before. (R.C.)

Purdie. There's something coming rushing back to me.

Mrs. Purdie. I seem to know that coffee-set. If I do, the lid of the milk-jug is chipped. (*She goes and examines it.*) It is.

Joanna (*now* R. *of* Lob's *chair, staring down at him*). I can't remember this man's name, but I am sure it begins with L.

Mrs. Purdie (*triumphantly*). Lob !

All. Lob !

(Joanna *comes down* L.C.)

Purdie (*above and* L. *of the table*). Mabel, your dress !

Mrs. Purdie (*looking down*). Gracious ! How on earth——!

Joanna. My dress ! (*To* Purdie.) You were in flannels in the wood.

Purdie. And so I am now. (*He looks down.*) Good heavens—— What's this ? Where did I change ? The wood ! Let me think ! (*Turning up to the windows, and then down* C., *above the table.*) The wood . . . the wood, certainly. But the wood wasn't the wood.

Joanna. My head's going round.

Mrs. Purdie. Lob's wood ! I remember it all ! (*She turns up* R.) We were here. We did go ! (*To* R. *of* Purdie.)

Purdie (*moving a little* L.C.). So we did ! But how could . . . ? Where was . . . ?

(*They speak almost simultaneously.*)

Joanna (*to* L. *of* Purdie). And who was . . . ?

Mrs. Purdie (*to* R. *of* Purdie). And what was . . . ?

Purdie (*excitedly, stretching a hand to each*). Don't let go. Hold on to what we were doing, or we'll lose grip of ourselves. (*Bewildered, passing his hands over his face.*) Devotion ! Some-

thing about devotion . . . Hold on to devotion . . . " If the
dog-like devotion of a lifetime . . ." (*Dropping his hands, and
looking from one to the other.*) Which of you was I saying
that to ?

MRS. PURDIE. To me.

PURDIE. Are you sure ?

MRS. PURDIE. I'm not quite sure.

PURDIE. Joanna ! What do you think ? Good heavens !
(*Sudden increase of uneasiness.*) Which of you is my wife ?

JOANNA. I am. (*Starts back a pace.*) No, I'm not.

PURDIE. What ?

JOANNA. It's Mabel who is your wife.

MRS. PURDIE (*retreating a little* R. *and down*). Me ?

(*They slowly take it in.*)

PURDIE. Why, of course you are, Mabel.

MRS. PURDIE. What ? I believe I am ! (*She sits* R. *of the
table.*)

PURDIE (*above the table*). How can it be ? I was running
away with you !

JOANNA. You needn't do it now. (*She sits* L. *of the table.*)

PURDIE (*almost with a grievance*). Why have I been making
all this fuss ? S-sh ! (*He turns a little up* C.) The wood . . .
hold on to the wood . . . it's the wood that explains it. Yes,
I see the whole thing. (*He gazes at* LOB.) You infernal old
rascal ! (*He shakes his fist at* LOB.) Let's try to think it out.
(*He sits above the table.*) Don't anyone speak for a moment.
Think first ! Love . . . ! Hold on to love. . . .

(*A pause, during which all three are very still. Then suddenly.*)

I say ! I believe I'm not a deeply passionate chap, at all !
I believe I'm just . . . a philanderer !

MRS. PURDIE (*nearly crying*). It's what you are ! You made
love to me in the wood, because you thought I wasn't your
wife. (*She rises, and crosses* R. *to the settee.*)

JOANNA. Mabel, what about ourselves ? I believe you and
I are both cats.

MRS. PURDIE. Speak for yourself, Joanna ! (*She sits* R.)

JOANNA. A pair of rank sentimentalists.

PURDIE. That's of no importance . . . Just a philanderer !
And if people don't change, I suppose we'll begin all over again
now !

JOANNA. I daresay, but not with each other. I may phil-
ander again—but not with you !

(*They look at each other, and give way to shame.*)

PURDIE (*rising*). Oh, John Purdie, John Purdie ! Barrister-

D

at-law ! (*He turns up* R. *of his chair, to* R.C.) The wood has taught me one thing, at any rate.

MRS. PURDIE. What, Jack ?

PURDIE. That it isn't accident that shapes our lives.

JOANNA. No, it's Fate.

PURDIE. It's not Fate, either. Fate is something outside us. What really plays the dickens with us is *something in ourselves*. Something that would make us go on doing the same sort of fool thing however many chances we get.

JOANNA. How ignominious ! But I believe you're right.

MRS. PURDIE. Can't we guide it ? Isn't that what we're here for ?

PURDIE. I daresay, if we try hard enough. But I have for the moment an abominably clear perception that the likes of me never really tries. I was just being the same twaddler over again ! Yes, I see it clearly now ; I'll forget it, I suppose, by morning. Forgive me, Joanna—no, Mabel . . . I'm mixed up still. (*He sits in the chair* R. *of the table.*)

JOANNA. I could forgive anybody anything to-night. It's so lovely not to be married to you, Jack !

PURDIE (*lugubrious*). I do feel small.

JOANNA. You'll soon swell up again.

PURDIE. That's the awful thing. But at present, at any rate, I am a rag at your feet, Joanna—no, at yours, Mabel. (*To* MRS. PURDIE.) Are you going to pick me up ?

MRS. PURDIE (*not to be mollified*). I don't know about that, Jack. To begin with, which of us is it your lonely soul is in search of ?

JOANNA. Which of us is the fluid one, or the fluider one ?

MRS. PURDIE. Are you and I one ? Or are you and Joanna one ? Or are the three of us two ?

JOANNA (*in burlesque of the sentimental lover*). He wants you to whisper in his ear the entrancing poem " Mabel Purdie." Do it, Mabel ! There will be nothing wrong in it now !

PURDIE (*rising, and crossing up* R.C.). Rub it in !

MRS. PURDIE (*firmly*). I understand you better now, Jack, at any rate. And when I meet Joanna's successor . . .

PURDIE (*quailing*). No, no, Mabel ! (*Earnestly, coming down* R.C.) There will never be another woman ! I swear it by all that's . . .

JOANNA (*in her excellent imitation of a sheep*). Baa ! He's off again ! (*She moves up* L. *to the fireplace recess.*)

(LOB *here—and once or twice later—indulges in his favourite kick.*)

PURDIE. Oh, Lord ! So I am ! (*He moves up to the chair* C.) In my present state of depression—which won't last—I feel there's something in me that will make me go on being eternally the same ass, however many chances I get. (*He rises from the arm of the chair*.) Shakespeare knew what he was talking about . . . (*Quoting*.)

> " The fault, dear Brutus, is not in our stars
> But in ourselves, that we are underlings."

JOANNA (*moving in a little towards* L.C.). For " dear Brutus " we are to read " dear audience ", I suppose ?

PURDIE. You have it. (*He moves* R.C., *between the table and the settee.*)

(JOANNA *sits* L. *of the table.*)

(*Sincere for the moment, moving towards the settee.*) Mabel, try to help me. If you catch me at it again, have the goodness to whisper to me in passing " Lob's Wood." That may cure me for the time being.

MRS. PURDIE (*sadly*). Perhaps I will . . . as long as I care to bother, Jack. It depends on you how long that is to be.

JOANNA. Hear, hear! There's hope in that as well as a warning. Perhaps the wood may prove to have been useful after all.

(*They are looking lugubrious.* PURDIE *turns to the chair* R. *of the table.*)

You know, we are not people worth being sorrowful about—so let's laugh !

(*They laugh, at first on the wrong side of their mouths, then heartily at themselves.*)

PURDIE (*pointing at* LOB). Queer ! I thought I saw him smile.

MRS. PURDIE (*suddenly, rising*). Stop ! I forgot. (*To* R.C.) JOANNA. What ?

MRS. PURDIE. We have forgotten the others. I wonder what is happening to them ?

PURDIE. By Jove, yes ! Have *they* changed ?

MRS. PURDIE. I didn't see any of them in the wood, did you ?

JOANNA. No. (*She rises.*) Or perhaps we did see them without knowing them. (*Turning up* C.) We didn't know Lob ! (*Looking at* LOB.)

PURDIE. That's true.

JOANNA (*turning to the others*). I say ! Won't it be delicious to be here to watch the others when they come back, and see them waking up, or whatever it was we did !

PURDIE. How do we know they'll come back ?

JOANNA (*startled*). We don't know ! (*To above the table.*) How awful ! (*She sits* C.)

MRS. PURDIE. Listen !

PURDIE. Sh-sh ! (*He moves down below the table.*) I distinctly hear someone on the stairs.

MRS. PURDIE. Matey ! (*She turns* R. *to the settee.*)

PURDIE (*turning back*). I say ! (*He moves* R. *of the table.*)

(MRS. PURDIE *sits on the settee.*)

Don't tell him we had any, any . . . odd experiences.

(*Enter* MRS. COADE, L., *in her dressing-gown with a muffler in her hand.*)

MRS. PURDIE (*rising*). It's Coady !

MRS. COADE. So you're back at last ! A nice house, I must say ! Where's Coady ? (*She goes up towards the window.*)

PURDIE. What ! (*Going up* C. *to meet* MRS. COADE.) Did he go into the wood, too ?

MRS. COADE. He must have. I've been down several times to look for him.

MRS. PURDIE. Coady, too !

JOANNA. I wonder . . . (*Suddenly, rising and moving* L.) Oh, how dreadful !

MRS. COADE (*coming down* R. *of* JOANNA). What is dreadful, Joanna ?

(MRS. PURDIE *sits* R., *on the settee.*)

JOANNA. Nothing. I was just wondering what he is doing.

MRS. COADE. Doing ? What should he be doing ? (*Looking from one to the other, moving to* C.) Did anything odd happen to you in the wood ?

(PURDIE *moves down* R.C.)

ALL (*hurriedly*). No, no, nothing.

JOANNA (*moving up* L.C.). We just strolled about and came back. (*Looking at* LOB.) Have you seen him ?

MRS. COADE. Oh, yes, he has been like that all the time. (*She sits above the table,* C.) A sort of stupor, I think, and sometimes the strangest grin comes over his face.

PURDIE. Grin ?

MRS. COADE. Just as if he were seeing amusing things in his sleep.

PURDIE (*behind the chair* R. *of the table*). And I daresay he is ! Oughtn't we to get Matey to him ?

MRS. COADE. Matey's gone, too.

PURDIE (*retreating a pace*). Wha-at ? (*He turns to look at* MRS. PURDIE, *and then moves up* R.)

MRS. PURDIE. Into the wood ?

MRS. COADE. I suppose so. He's not in the house.

JOANNA (*coming down* L.C.). Matey ! (*Looking across at* PURDIE.) I wonder who's with him ?

MRS. COADE (*anxious*). Must somebody be with him ?
JOANNA. Oh, no, not at all.

(*There is a knock at the window. They all look in that direction.*)

MRS. COADE. Listen ! I hope it's Coady.
MRS. PURDIE (*sorry for her, rising.*) Oh, I hope not !
MRS. COADE. Why, Mrs. Purdie ?

(*Going up above* MRS. COADE'S *chair and bending over.*)

JOANNA. Dear Mrs. Coade, whoever he is with and whatever
he does, I beg you not to be surprised. We feel that though
we had no unusual experiences in the wood, others may not have
been so fortunate.
MRS. PURDIE (*moving to* R. *of* MRS. COADE). And be cautious,
you dear, what you say to them before they come to.
MRS. COADE. " Come to " ? You alarm me. And Coady
didn't have his muffler.

(JOANNA *moves down* L. *of the table.* PURDIE *goes up to* R. *of the
windows and peeps out.* MRS. PURDIE *moves down* R. *to the settee.*
MRS. COADE *pushes her chair slightly* L., *turned to face* R., *as*
PURDIE *draws back.*)

PURDIE. Sh-sh ! (*Coming to* R.C.) Matey ! (*He moves to
above the settee and sits.*)

(MATEY *enters at the windows* C. *Though in his butler's clothes—
of which he is unaware—he retains his aggressive business-man
manner.*)

JOANNA. Do come in !
MATEY. With apologies, ladies and gents . . . May I ask
who is host ?
PURDIE (*seated on the upper arm of the settee*). A very reason-
able request. Third on the left. (*He points delightedly to* LOB,
and turns R., *above the settee.*)
MATEY (*crossing to* R. *of* LOB'S *chair*). Only to ask, sir, if
you would direct me to my hotel. I . . . the gentleman seems
to be reposing. (*He returns to* R.C.)
MRS. COADE. It's Lob !
MATEY (R. *of* MRS. COADE). What is Lob, ma'am ? . . .
MRS. COADE. Surely you haven't forgotten !
PURDIE. Sh-sh ! Anything we can do for you ? Just give
it a name.
JOANNA. I hope you are not alone. Do you say have some
lady friend with you.
MATEY. My wife is with me.
JOANNA. His wife ! You *have* been quick !
MRS. PURDIE. I am so glad ! I love a bride !
MRS. COADE. I didn't know you were married !

MATEY. Why should you ? You talk as if you knew me

MRS. COADE. Good gracious ! Do you really think I don't ?

(MATEY *stares at* MRS. COADE.)

PURDIE. Sit down, won't you, and make yourself comfy ?

MATEY. Thank you, but my wife . . .

JOANNA. Yes, please bring her in. We are simply dying to make her acquaintance.

MATEY. You are very good. I'm much obliged. (*He exits* C.)

MRS. PURDIE (*crossing up to* R. *of the windows*). Who can she be ? (*She comes* C.)

JOANNA. Who ? Who ? Who ?

MRS. COADE (*rising*). But what an extraordinary wood ! (*She moves to* L. *of the table.*) He doesn't seem to know who he is at all.

MRS. PURDIE. Don't worry about that, Coady. He will know soon enough. (*She turns up to the windows and peeps out, through the curtains.*)

JOANNA. And so will the little wife. (*Moving up* C., *to* L. *of the windows.*) By the way, whoever she is, I hope she's fond of butlers.

MRS. PURDIE (*peeping through window*). It's Lady Caroline ! (*She hurries back down* R.)

JOANNA (*following* MRS. PURDIE *down* R.) Oh, hurray ! And she was so sure she couldn't take the wrong turning !

(*They both stand down* R., *in front of the settee, as* MATEY *and* LADY CAROLINE *enter* C. LADY CAROLINE *is all graciousness.*)

MATEY (*on her* L.). May I present my wife—Lady Caroline Matey.

PURDIE (*crossing to* R. *of* LADY CAROLINE). How do you do, Lady Caroline ?

MRS. COADE (*aghast*). Lady Caroline Matey ! You !

LADY CAROLINE. Charmed, I'm sure.

(MRS. COADE *sits above the table* C.)

JOANNA. Very pleased to meet any wife of Mr. Matey.

PURDIE (R.C.). Allow me. (*Introducing* MRS. COADE.) The Duchess of Candelabra. (*Introducing* JOANNA *and* MRS. PURDIE.) The Ladies Helena and Matilda McNab. I am Mr. Justice Purdie.

LADY CAROLINE. How d'you do ? How d'y' do ! (*She sits* R. *of the table.*)

MRS. PURDIE (*sitting on lower end of the settee*). I have wanted so long to make your acquaintance.

LADY CAROLINE. Charmed !

JOANNA. These informal meetings are so delightful . . . don't you . . . ? (*She sits on the upper end of the settee.*)

LADY CAROLINE. Yes, indeed !

MATEY (*looking at* LOB). And your friend by the fire ?

PURDIE. I'll introduce you to him when you wake up—I mean when he wakes up. (*He sits on the upstage arm of the settee.*)

MATEY. Perhaps I ought to have said that I am *James* Matey.

LADY CAROLINE. *The* James Matey.

MATEY. A name not perhaps unknown in the world of finance.

JOANNA. Finance ! Oh ! So you did take that clerkship in the city ?

MATEY. I began as a clerk in the city, certainly, and I'm not ashamed to admit it.

MRS. COADE (*muddled with wonder*). Fancy that, now. And did it save you ?

MATEY. Save me, madam ?

JOANNA. Excuse us—we ask odd questions in this house— we only mean, did that keep you honest ? Or are you still a pilferer ?

LADY CAROLINE (*to* MATEY). Husband mine ! What does she mean ?

JOANNA. No offence. I mean a pilferer on a large scale.

MATEY (*blustering, to* R.C.). If you are referring to that Labrador business—or the Working Women's Bank . . .

PURDIE. O-oh ! Got him !

JOANNA (*delighted*). Yes, those are what I meant !

MATEY (*stoutly*). There was nothing proved.

JOANNA (*rising*). Mabel ! Jack ! Here's another of us. (*She goes up to* MATEY.) You've gone just the same way, again, my friend ! There's more in it, you see, than taking the wrong turning ! *You* would always take the wrong turning. Tra-la-la !

(JOANNA *trips back to the settee.* LADY CAROLINE *rises and goes up,* R.C.)

LADY CAROLINE. If you are casting any aspersions on my husband, allow me to say that a prouder wife than I does not to-day exist.

MRS. COADE. My dear, do be careful.

MRS. PURDIE (*down* R.). So long as *you* are satisfied, dear Lady Caroline ! But I thought you hated all men, and had a contempt for love.

LADY CAROLINE (*indignant*). I ? I beg to assure you that I adore my Jim. (*She turns to* MATEY, *her hand on his arm.*)

JOANNA (*to* MRS. PURDIE). Jim !

(*They are amused.*)

(*But* MATEY *has come upon the tray containing the coffee-cups.*

He lifts it and moves about L.C. *with it puzzled, but in correct butler manner.*)

LADY CAROLINE (*moving towards him.*) Whatever are you doing, Jim ?

(*There is a pause. Then :*)

MATEY. I don't understand it, Caroliney, but somehow I feel at home with this in my hands !

MRS. PURDIE. Caroliney !

MRS. COADE. Look at me well. Don't you remember **me** ?

MATEY (*staring at her*). I don't remember you ; but I seem to associate you with hard-boiled eggs. (*With conviction, putting down the tray.*) You like your eggs hard-boiled ?

PURDIE (*crossing to* R.C.). Hold on to hard-boiled eggs. She used to tip you especially to see to them ! (*He crosses to* MATEY.)

(MATEY'S *hand goes to his pocket.*)

Yes, that was the pocket.

LADY CAROLINE (*indignantly*). Tip ? James ? (*She comes down* R.C.)

MATEY (*dwelling pleasantly on the word*). Tip !

(LADY CAROLINE *is looking around.*)

PURDIE. Jolly word, isn't it ?

MATEY. It seems to set me thinking.

LADY CAROLINE (*crosses to the desk* L.—*suddenly seeing it*). Why is my work-basket in this house ?

MRS. COADE. You are living here, you know.

(JOANNA *and* MRS. PURDIE *rise* slowly.)

LADY CAROLINE (*to* L.C.). That's what a person feels. But when did I come ? It's very odd, but one feels one ought to say when did one go.

PURDIE. She's coming to with a " wush " !

MATEY (*up* C.). Mr. . . . Purdie !

LADY CAROLINE. Mrs. Coade !

MATEY (*turning to look at* LOB). The guv'nor.

LADY CAROLINE. One is in evening dress !

MATEY. Oh, Moses !

(*They are startled by their clothes.*)

JOANNA. You will understand clearly in a minute, Caroliney. You didn't really take that clerkship, Jim. You went into domestic service. But in the essentials you haven't altered.

PURDIE (*to up* R.C.). I'll have my shaving water at seven-thirty sharp, Matey. (*He turns back to* MRS. PURDIE.)

MATEY (*in servant manner*). Very good, sir. (*His hands stray unconsciously to the tray.*)

LADY CAROLINE (*crossing to* L. *of* MATEY). Sir ! You . . .
You . . . You . . . Midsummer Eve ! The wood.
PURDIE (*turning to her*). Yes, hold on to the wood.
MATEY. You are . . . you are . . . you are Lady Caroline
Laney.
LADY CAROLINE. It's Matey, the butler !
MRS. PURDIE. You seem quite happy with him, you know,
Lady Caroline.
JOANNA (*nicely*). We won't tell.

(*A pause.* PURDIE *sits on the upstage arm of the settee.*)

LADY CAROLINE. Caroline Matey ! And I seem to like it !
(*A pause of horror.*) How horrible.

(LADY CAROLINE *sits abruptly,* L. *of the table.* MATEY *is be-*
wildered.)

MRS. COADE. It's rather difficult to see what we should do
next !
MATEY (*superbly controlling himself, the tray still in his hands.*
To LADY CAROLINE L.). Coffee, my Lady ?
LADY CAROLINE (*also rather superb*). No !

(*A pause.*)

MATEY (*tentatively*). Perhaps if I were to go downstairs ?
PURDIE. It would be conferring a personal favour on us all.

(MATEY *crosses down* L. *correctly with the tray, and exits.*)

(NOTE.—*The cake on the plate has been left on the table.*)

(LOB *again gives his kick.*)

LADY CAROLINE (*rising, and going up* L. *to the* R. *of* LOB'S *chair*).
It's all that wretch's doing. . . .

(LADY CAROLINE *shakes his chair, but* LOB *does not waken. The*
playing of COADE'S *whistle is heard off.*)

JOANNA (*up at the window, and peeping*). It's Coady !

(JOANNA *goes down* L. *of the chair* C. LADY CAROLINE *to* L.C.)

MRS. COADE (*rising*). Coady ! (*Moving to* R.C.) Why is he
so happy ? (*She moves, troubled, to the settee,* R., *and sits.*)
JOANNA (*moving down to* MRS. COADE). Dear, take my hand.

(JOANNA *sits* L. *of* MRS. COADE, *taking her left hand.* MRS.
PURDIE *takes her right hand ; they are both very nice to her.*
She looks from one to the other. LADY CAROLINE *sits* L. *of the*
table.)

(*To* L. *of* MRS. COADE.) Dear, hold my hand. (*She takes* MRS.
COADE'S *left hand.*)

(MRS. COADE *sits on the sofa. They are both very nice to her.*)

MRS. COADE. Won't he know me ?
JOANNA (*apprehensive, still holding* MRS. COADE'S *hand*). Oh dear, I wish Coady hadn't gone out.

(PURDIE *moves to behind the settee.*)

MRS. COADE. We that have been happily married these thirty years.

(COADE *comes in inquiringly with a skip and jump, wearing his Act I clothes like the others.*)

COADE (*up* R.C.). May I intrude ? My name is Coade. The fact is I was playing about in the wood on a whistle, and I saw your light.

(*The others uncomfortably let* MRS. COADE *have most to say.*)

MRS. COADE. Playing about in the wood with a whistle ! You !
COADE (*moving down a pace, with mild dignity*). And why not, madam ?
MRS. COADE. Madam ! (*Wistful.*) Don't you know me ?
COADE (*taking a pace or two towards her down* R.). I don't know you . . . (*Looking at her.*) But I wish I did.
MRS. COADE. Do you ? Why ?
COADE. If I may say so, you have a very soft, lovable face.

(MRS. COADE *looks at the others with the smile of a pleased child. They nod encouragingly.* JOANNA *gives her hand a reassuring pat, rises quietly and moves up, and across to above the chair* R. *of the table.*)

MRS. COADE. Who was with you playing whistles in the wood !

(*Everybody is very tense.*)

COADE. No one was with me.

(*General relaxation.*)

MRS. COADE. No . . . lady ?
COADE. Certainly not !

(MRS. COADE *beams.*)

(*Moving nearer the upper end of the settee.*) I am a bachelor.
MRS. COADE (*quaking*). A bachelor ?
JOANNA (*moving to* R. *of the* R. *chair*). Don't give way, dear ! It—might—be much worse.
MRS. COADE. And you're sure you never spoke to me before ? Do think !

COADE. Not to my knowledge. Never . . . except in dreams.

MRS. PURDIE. What did you say to her in dreams?

COADE (*reflecting*). I said, "My dear." (*He is surprised himself.*) Odd!

JOANNA. The darling man!

MRS. COADE (*trembling*). How could you say such things to an old woman?

COADE. Old? (*Puzzled.*) I didn't think of you as old. No, no! Young! With the morning dew on your face, coming across the lawn in a black and green silk dress, and such a pretty parasol.

MRS. COADE. That was how he first met me. He used to love me in black and green. And it was a pretty parasol. Look! I'm old. So it can't be the same woman.

COADE. Old! Yes, I suppose so. But it is the same soft, lovable face, and the same kind beaming smile that children could warm their hands at.

MRS. COADE (*with a child's smile to the others*). He always liked my smile.

(*There is a tiny pause.*)

PURDIE. So do we all.

COADE. Emma!

MRS. COADE. He hasn't forgotten my name. (*To the others.*)

COADE. It's sad that we didn't meet long ago. I think I've been waiting for you. I suppose we have met too late? You couldn't overlook my being an old fellow, could you? No!

JOANNA. How lovely! (*She turns up* C., *to above the table.*) He is going to propose to her again! Coady, you happy thing! He is wanting the same soft face after thirty years. (*She sits* C.)

MRS. COADE (*after beaming again*). We mustn't be too sure. I think that's it. I hope it is. Perhaps I'm wrong, Joanna. What is it exactly you want, *Mr*. Coade?

COADE. I want to have the right to hold the parasol over you. Won't you be my wife, my dear? And so give my long dream of you a happy ending?

(MRS. COADE *rises and smooths his arms, then looking triumphantly at the others.*)

MRS. COADE. Kisses are not called for at our age, Coady, but here's a muffler for your old neck.

COADE (*simply*). Thank you, dear, I've missed it. (*He is tying it in a matter-of-fact way round his neck when he becomes conscious of his evening clothes. He looks round him, blinking.*) Why . . . why . . . what . . . who . . . how is this? (*He wanders up* R.C.)

PURDIE. He's coming to!

COADE (*looking at the chair, then remembering, after an effort, in which the others are in suspense*). Lob !

(LOB *gives his kick.*)

PURDIE. You've got it, old man !

COADE (*returning down* R. *to* MRS. COADE). Bless me, Coady ! I went into that wood.

MRS. COADE. And without your muffler.

(MRS. COADE *sits on the settee, and then notices* COADE *is feeling his pockets.*

What are you feeling for ?

COADE (*up* C.). The whistle ! Gone ! Of course it is ! It's rather a pity, but . . . (*Anxiously coming to* R.C.) Have I been saying awful things to you ?

MRS. PURDIE. You have been making her so proud. You had a second chance, and it's her again.

COADE. Of course ! It would be ! But I see I was just the same nice old lazy Coady as before ! And I had thought that if I had a second chance I could *do* things ! I've often said to you, Coady, that it was owing to my being cursed with a competency that I didn't write my great book. But I had no competency this time, and I haven't written a word.

PURDIE (*to* R. *of* COADE, *with a fellow feeling*). That needn't make you feel lonely in this house.

(MRS. PURDIE *rises and turns down and behind the settee.*)

MRS. COADE. You seem to have been quite happy as an old bachelor, dear !

COADE. I'm surprised at myself, but I'm afraid I was.

MRS. COADE. I wonder if what it means is that you don't especially need even me. I wonder if it means that you are just the sort of amiable creature that would be happy anywhere and anyhow.

COADE. Oh dear, can it be as bad as that ?

JOANNA. Certainly not ! It's a romance, and I won't have it looked upon as anything else.

(PURDIE *moves up to the windows.*)

MRS. COADE. Thank you, Joanna. You'll try not to miss that whistle, Coady !

COADE (*moving towards* MRS. COADE). Not while I have your smile to make the music for me, Emma. You are all I need. (*Kissing her hand.*)

MRS. COADE. Yes, but I'm not so sure as I used to be that it's a great compliment.

JOANNA. Coady, behave ! (*She rises and turns up* L.)

(*There is a knock at the window.* LADY CAROLINE *rises.* PURDIE
goes up and peeps out.)

PURDIE (*turning to the others*).   Mrs. Dearth—alone !

(LADY CAROLINE *turns* L. *to the desk,* JOANNA *drops down above
and on her* R.)

(*Moving to* L.C.)   Who would have expected it of *her* !

(COADE *moves to* R. *of the windows.*)

JOANNA.   She's rather a dear, and I do hope she's got off
cheaply.

(COADE *moves across to* R. *of* PURDIE.
MRS. DEARTH *enters at the windows, in her evening dress and
cloak.   She simpers to show that she is the equal of these fine
ladies.*)

PURDIE.   Pleased to see you, stranger !
MRS. DEARTH (C.).   I was afraid such an unceremonious
entry might startle you.
PURDIE.   Not a bit.
MRS. DEARTH.   I usually enter a house by the front
door.
PURDIE.   I've heard that's the swagger way.
MRS. DEARTH.   So stupid of me, I lost myself in the wood . . .
and . . .
JOANNA.   Of course you did, but never mind that.   Do tell
us your name.
LADY CAROLINE.   Yes, yes, your name !
MRS. DEARTH.   Of course.   I'm the Honourable Mrs. Finch-
Fallowe.
MRS. PURDIE.   Of course, of course.
LADY CAROLINE.   Who can he be ?
PURDIE.   I hope Mr. Finch-Fallowe is very well.   We don't
know him personally ; but may we have the pleasure of seeing
him pop in presently ?
MRS. DEARTH.   No, I'm not sure where he is.
LADY CAROLINE.   I wonder if the dear clever police
know ?
MRS. DEARTH.   No, they don't !
PURDIE.   Phew !
MRS. DEARTH.   So awkward !   I gave my sandwiches to a
poor girl and her father whom I met in the wood, and now . . .
(*Faltering.*)   Isn't that a nuisance ?   I'm quite hungry myself.
(*Seeing the cake.*)   May I ?   (*She sits* R. *of the table, and falls
to without waiting for permission.   She wolfs the cake.*)
MRS. COADE.   The poor thing !

PURDIE (*moving to* C., *above the table, referring to the cake*). Like it ?

MRS. DEARTH. Delicious !

(COADE *closes in to* L. *of* PURDIE, *at* L.C. JOANNA *moves in below and* L. *of* COADE. LADY CAROLINE *rises and moves in a pace.*)

JOANNA (*to* LADY CAROLINE). Finch-Fallowe.

LADY CAROLINE. Dear Mrs. Finch-Fallowe, we are so anxious to know whether you met a friend of ours in the wood—a Mr. Dearth ? Perhaps you know him, too ?

MRS. DEARTH. Dearth ? I don't know any Dearth.

MRS. COADE. Oh dear ! What a wood !

(MRS. PURDIE *moves to* L. *of the upper end of the settee.*)

PURDIE. He is quite a front-door sort of man. Knocks and rings as cool as you like.

MRS. DEARTH. I meet so many, you see, and go out a great deal. I have visiting-cards—printed ones.

(LADY CAROLINE *turns and sits at the desk.*)

MRS. PURDIE (*moving a pace towards* MRS. DEARTH). Perhaps he has painted your portrait ? He is an artist.

MRS. DEARTH (*over her shoulder*). Very likely. (*Eating.*) I daresay that is the man I gave my sandwiches to.

MRS. COADE. But I thought you said *he* had a daughter.

MRS. DEARTH. Such a pretty girl ! I gave her half a crown.

COADE. A daughter ! (*Looking from one to the other.*) That can't be Dearth.

PURDIE. Don't be too sure. (*To* MRS. DEARTH.) A rather melancholy, gone-to-seed sort of man ?

MRS. DEARTH. No, I thought him such a jolly attractive man.

COADE. Dearth, jolly attractive ? Oh, no ! (*Coming a little down* L.) Did he say anything about his wife ?

LADY CAROLINE. Yes, do try to remember if he mentioned *her ?*

MRS. DEARTH. No, he didn't. (COADE *moves up below the fireplace.*)

PURDIE. He was far from jolly in her time.

MRS. DEARTH (*simpering*). Perhaps that was the lady's fault. (*She goes on eating.*)

(PURDIE *is amused, and crosses to* R. *of* COADE. DEARTH *is heard singing a French song off.* MRS. PURDIE *moves down* R., *and sits above* MRS. COADE.)

COADE. Dearth singing. He seems quite gay !

JOANNA (*moving up to* L. *of* MRS. DEARTH). You poor thing !

PURDIE. H'sh ! H'sh !

(JOANNA *moves* R., *to above and* L. *of the settee.* DEARTH *comes in at the windows dressed as at end of Act I.* PURDIE *and* COADE *are at* L., *below the fireplace.*)

DEARTH (*still a happy man*). I'm sorry to bounce in on you in this way, but really I have an excuse. I'm a painter of sorts, and . . .

(*He checks, up* C., *seeing that he has brought some strange discomfort here.*)

MRS. COADE. I must say, Mr. Dearth, I am delighted to see you looking so well. Like a new man, isn't he ?

(*No one dares to answer. Glances are exchanged.*)

DEARTH. I'm certainly very well, if you care to know. But did I tell you my name ?

JOANNA (*turning up* R.C. *to* DEARTH). No, but we have an instinct in this house.

DEARTH (*facing* JOANNA). Well, it doesn't matter. Here's the situation. My daughter and I have just met in the wood a poor wretched woman famishing for want of food.

(*Here* MRS. DEARTH *rises slowly, and backs below and to* R. *of her chair.*)

We were as happy as grigs ourselves, and the sight of her distress rather cut us up. Can you give me something for her ? (*Checking.*) Why are you looking so startled ? (*He turns to the table and sees the remains of the cake.*) May I have this ?

(*A slight movement from* MRS. DEARTH *attracts his attention, and for the first time he sees her. He recognizes her as the woman in the wood and her dress astonishes him. The others are beginning to understand the situation. He frowns, and takes a step* R.C. *towards her.*)

I feel I can't be mistaken. It *was* you I met in the wood. Have you been playing some trick on me ? (*To the others.*) It was for her I wanted the food.

MRS. DEARTH (*putting her hand to her dress, to protect his gift*). Are you going to take back the money you gave me ?

DEARTH. Your dress ! You were almost in rags when I saw you outside.

(MRS. DEARTH *looks down and is startled by her attire.*)

MRS. DEARTH. I don't . . . understand . . .

COADE (*crossing* PURDIE *to up* L.C.). For that matter, Dearth, I daresay you were different in the wood, too.

DEARTH (*he becomes aware of his dress clothes*). What . . . What . . . Am I crazy ?

MRS. DEARTH (*looking around, bewildered and no longer a*

comedy figure). Where am I ? I seem to know you . . . (*She crosses to* MRS. COADE, *down* R.)

MRS. COADE (*kindly*). Yes, you do. Hold my hand, and you'll soon remember all about it.

JOANNA (*moving a pace or two to* DEARTH, *kindly*). I'm afraid, Mr. Dearth, it's harder for you than the rest of us.

MRS. PURDIE (*seated down* R.). We're awfully sorry. Don't you remember . . . Midsummer Eve !

(COADE *turns slowly back to* PURDIE *up* L.)

DEARTH. Midsummer Eve ! This room ! Yes, this room . . . You . . . was it you . . . were going out to look for something . . . The tree of knowledge, wasn't it ? Somebody wanted me to go, too . . . Who was it ? A lady, I think . . . Why did she ask me to go ? What was I doing here ? I was smoking a cigar . . . I laid it down, there . . . (*He goes straight to the ashtray stand up* R., *where he had put his cigar, and lifts it up. He looks around, puts it back on the stand, and shivers a little.*) Who was the lady ? (*He moves to* R.C.)

MRS. DEARTH (*slowly—staring out front*). Something about a second chance.

MRS. COADE. Yes, you poor dear. You thought you could make so much of it.

DEARTH. A lady who didn't like me . . . she had good reasons, too ; but what were they . . . ?

MRS. DEARTH (*swinging round to face* L.). Lob ! He did it ! (*To* R.C.) What did he do ?

DEARTH (*a tragic figure*). I'm . . . it's coming back ! (*To above the table* C.) I'm not the man I thought myself . . .

MRS. DEARTH. I'm not Mrs. Finch-Fallowe ! Who am I ?

(*The husband and wife stare at each other, and then realize.*)

DEARTH (*to above the chair* R. *of the table*). You were that lady !

MRS. DEARTH (*retreating a step* R.). It's you—my husband !

DEARTH. Alice !

(*There is very little movement, but they are overcome.*)

MRS. COADE. My dear, you are much better off, so far as I can see, than if you *were* Mrs. Finch-Fallowe.

MRS. DEARTH (*generously*). Yes. (*With passionate knowledge.*) Yes, indeed ! *But he isn't !*

DEARTH (*taking a step down towards* MRS. DEARTH). Alice . . . I . . . (*He tries to smile.*) I didn't know you when I was in the wood with Margaret ! She . . . she . . . (*He realizes his greatest loss.*) Margaret ! Oh, my God !

(DEARTH *sits* R. *of the table burying his face in his hands. No one can do anything.* MRS. DEARTH *goes to him. A pause.*)

MRS. DEARTH. I should have liked to have been her mother, Will.

(*He does not look up. She presses his shoulder fiercely and goes out* L. *He remains with his head in his hands ; the others don't know what to do.*)

PURDIE (*below and* L. *of* LOB'S *chair*). You old ruffian ! ! !
DEARTH (*looking up*). No, I'm rather fond of him. (*Rising.*) Our lonely, friendly little host. (*Crosses up* L. *to* R. *of* LOB'S *chair.*) Lob, I thank thee for that hour ! (*He goes down and opens the door* L., *pauses, and calls.*) Alice !

(DEARTH *goes out* L., *closing the door.*)

JOANNA (*moving to the table*). If one could only change ! (*She sits in the chair* R. *of the table.*)
MRS. PURDIE (*rising*). Who knows ? Perhaps the brave ones can. (*Moving up* R.C.) You know I feel sorry for her, as well as for him.
JOANNA. She's really quite a good sort.
PURDIE (*moving across up* C.). I daresay there's nothing the matter with her except that she would always choose the wrong man. Good man or bad ; but the wrong man for her. I think we had best all toddle off to bed. Hold on to bed.

(LADY CAROLINE *rises, moving to* L. *of the table. All brighten up.*)

MRS. PURDIE. And try a little reflection before we fall asleep.
COADE. Yes, yes ! (*Crossing to above the table.*) It must be quite late !
MRS. COADE. That's my candle, Coady.

(COADE *lights the candle.* MATEY *enters from the dining-room, up* R.)

MATEY. Breakfast is quite ready.

(*There is pleasant excitement.*)

ALL. Breakfast ! Breakfast !

(MRS. COADE *rises and moves up.*)

LADY CAROLINE (*looking at her watch*). My watch has stopped.
COADE (*looking at his*). And mine.
JOANNA. Just as well, perhaps. (*She rises and goes up.*)
COADE (*moving across* R.C.). You know, now that I think of it, I feel quite peckish !
MRS. COADE. There's a smell of coffee.

(*They go towards the dining-room.*)

COADE (*taking her arm*). Come along, Coady ! I do hope you haven't been tiring your poor foot too much !

MRS. COADE. I shall give it a good rest to-morrow, dear.

MATEY (*as they pass*). I have given your egg six minutes, ma'am.

(MR. *and* MRS. COADE *exit* R.)

(PURDIE *exits with* MRS. PURDIE *to the dining-room.*

LADY CAROLINE *crosses up* R. *She and* MATEY *have a self-conscious look at each other; getting in each other's way. He draws aside, and* LADY CAROLINE *goes out* R. *and closes the door.*)

JOANNA (*reflectively coming down to above the table*). A strange experience! (*She calls.*) Matey.

MATEY. Yes, miss? (*Coming* C.)

JOANNA. Does it ever have any permanent effect, Matey?

MATEY. Not often, miss, but once in a while. If you want to know whether it will have any on you, he could show you if he liked.

JOANNA. Catch me risking it! (*She turns* R.) But I should like to know about the Dearths. Breakfast!

(*She exits* R.)

MATEY (*setting the chairs into the table*). Did you hear what the lady said, you mischievous, innocent old devil? . . .

(LOB *kicks, and withdraws his leg from view.* MATEY *goes to his chair and seizes it, leaning well over it as he speaks.*)

You've diddled me again and again, but I think I've got you now. . . .

(NOTE.—*During the above line and bus.,* LOB *makes a trick exit through the wall above the chair.*)

(MATEY *pulls the chair round to face down, and finds it empty. He shakes his head tolerantly as one who knows* LOB'S *ways, then switches off the lights. He then goes up and draws aside the curtains.*

We now see the garden in full daylight. LOB *is standing there with his back to us. He jumps round to startle* MATEY, *who goes off to the dining-room with a tolerant smile.*

LOB *remembers what* JOANNA *had said about wanting to know the future of the* DEARTHS. *He works a spell with his hands. A lark is heard singing in the garden.* LOB *hides behind the curtain, retreating to* L. *of the windows.*

DEARTH *in a tweed suit, carrying easel and canvas, humming a French song and smoking a pipe, happy again, comes into view. He looks up at the lark and smiles. He beckons, and* MRS. DEARTH *comes, dressed rather like* MARGARET. *They look happily at each other, kiss and pass on. There is a moment's pause and then* MARGARET, *as she was in the wood, gaily dances after them. The lark sings on.* LOB, *looking very old, but pleased, sinks into his chair and has a final kick. But he is really very tired of it all. Perhaps he is a sprite who has lost his way among the mortals.*

CURTAIN.

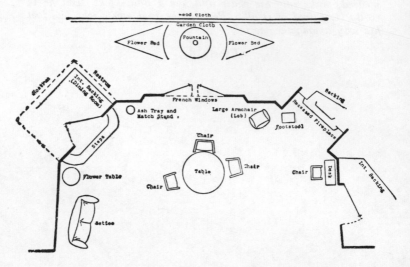

FURNITURE AND PROPERTY PLOT

ACT I

Carpet on the stage.
3 rugs (at the fireplace, the windows, and below the steps).
Garden cloth in the exterior.
Fountain, rose trees, etc., in the exterior setting.
Set built trees when cloth is changed, striking all garden features.)

Interior Setting.
  Carpet on the stage.
  3 rugs (at the fireplace, the windows, and below the steps).
  Round table (C.).

  On the Table.—Cigar box (with cigars).
    Ashtray.
    2 or 3 novels. Periodicals.
    Bowl of roses.
  3 drawing-room chairs (with arms) around C. table.
  Settee (down R.).
  Small table (R. above the settee).

  On the above.—Bowl of roses.
    Glass jug of water.
  Writing desk (L.).
  Chair at the above.

  On the Desk.—Blotter, stationery, inkstand, telegraph forms.
  Deep high-backed armchair (up L. of the windows, to face the garden).
  Footstool (in the fireplace recess).
  Ashtray and matchstand (up R. of the windows).

  On the Mantel.—Clock. Two or three small figures, or ornaments.

68

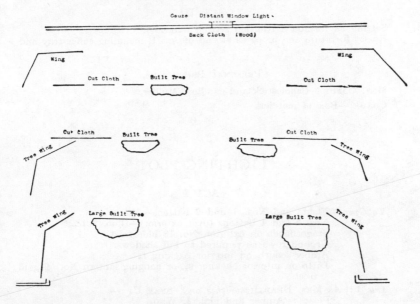

Gauze   Distant Window Light

Back Cloth   (Wood)

Wing   Wing

Cut Cloth   Built Tree   Cut Cloth

Cut Cloth   Built Tree   Built Tree   Cut Cloth

Tree Wing   Tree Wing

Tree Wing   Large Built Tree   Large Built Tree   Tree Wing

PERSONAL PROPERTIES

MATEY (*off* L.).—Tray with 5 coffee-cups and saucers, etc., plate with cake, and lidded milk-jug.
Five ladies' rings (*in waistcoat pocket*).

DEARTH.—Cigar, matches.

(NOTE : Ready off L., cloaks and wraps for ladies.)

ACT II

Stage cloth, for wood.
Built trees as shown in Ground Plan.
Strewn on ground.—Leaves, twigs, small boughs.

PERSONAL PROPERTIES

MATEY.—Travelling rug.
Cigar-case and cigars.
Matches.
Coins (in trousers pockets).

PURDIE.—Old waterproof coat.

COADE (*To bring on for whistle*).—Small bough.
(Another, similar, on stage for dance.)

DEARTH.—Low portable easel. Paint-box, palette, brushes.
Pipe. Tobacco pouch. Matches, in R. pocket of jacket.
Ten-shilling note.

MARGARET.—Hair-ribbon, hair-clips. Pieces of biscuit.

ACT III

Setting as for Act I (Garden setting exterior).
Re-set furniture and props as at end of Act I, including coffee-tray and cake.

PERSONAL PROPERTIES.

MRS. COADE.—Candlestick and candle. Muffler.
COADE.—Box of matches.

LIGHTING PLOT

ACT I

To Open.—Floats and Nos. 1 and 2 battens—*Nil.*
Nos. 3 and 4 battens (over exterior)—Blue, FULL.
Stage floods on exterior, No. 18 blue frost.
Ground rows as required to kill shadows.
Amber length on interior backing L.
Ditto on interior backing R., or hanging lantern No. 52 gold frost.

Cue 1: *As* MRS. DEARTH *switches on:* SNAP UP:—
Floats: Amber and pink ½, White ¼.
Nos. 1 and 2 battens: Amber and pink ¾, white ½.
All stage fittings ON.
Acting area lantern (if available), No. 52 gold, over C.

Cue 2: LOB. "It's quite a flirtation, isn't it?".—Commence very slow change of stage floods to No. 19 frost and ground rows to *Nil.* Exterior battens to ½.

Cue 3: *After* MRS. PURDIE *has drawn the curtains across* (*when the wood exterior is set to replace garden*).—Change exterior floods to No. 16 moonlight blue, and take OUT blue in battens. (Set floods to kill all shadows on cloth.)

Cue 4: *As* LOB *switches off.*—SNAP OUT all lighting on interior set. No change on exterior.

ACT II

To Open.—Floats, blue only, at ¼, No. 1 batten, blue only, ½.

Cue 1: *During opening "nightingale".*—Slowly bring up blue in floats to ½, and amber ¼. No. 1 batten, blue FULL, amber ½. No. 3 batten, blue only at ½. No. 4 (if used), blue only at ¼. Follow with batten spot set between C. and R., No. 16 or No. 18 blue frost, directed to C. acting area, at ½.

Cue 2: JOANNA. "That's all you know—you bird." (*Exit.*)—Bring up moon spot to FULL. (About 1 minute.)

Cue 3: DEARTH. "I can't get her out of my mind."—Fade out all amber in floats and battens (½ min.). At the same time, check all blues slowly to *Nil* at curtain fall, and moon spot to ½.

Cue 4: *As* DEARTH *packs up.*—Bring in distant house light effect behind gauze on cloth. Check this as indicated in the script.

Cue 5 : When MARGARET runs up stage in panic, the distant house effect should be OUT. Also all floats and battens, and moon spot to ½. This latter should be down to ¼ when she returns down to the tree R.

Cue 6 : MARGARET. " I don't want to be a might-have-been."—Quick fade out of moon spot, and Curtain fall.

ACT III

To Open.—Interior—BLACK OUT.
Exterior—One batten, blue, only at ¼.
Amber length in interior backing.
No lighting in dining-room backing.

Cue 1 : *As* PURDIE switches on.—SNAP ON all lighting as in Act I— interior setting *only*.

Cue 2 : PURDIE. " . . . Hold on to bed."—Lengths ON in dining-room.

Cue 3 : *As* MATEY *switches off.*—SNAP OUT all lighting on interior setting, except amber in floats *only*, at ¼.

(NOTE.—Before Cue 3 the battens on exterior are brought in amber, pink, and white FULL, and stage floods on the exterior setting mingled straw and No. 17 steel blue, both frost. This change is made while the curtains are still closed.)

DEAR BRUTUS

A Comedy in Three Acts

by

J. M. BARRIE

This Acting Edition of "Dear Brutus"
is published by permission of
Messrs. Hodder and Stoughton Ltd.

SAMUEL FRENCH

FRENCH

LONDON

NEW YORK SYDNEY TORONTO HOLLYWOOD

Printed in Great Britain
Photo-litho reprint by W & J Mackay Limited, Chatham
From earlier impression